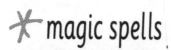

*magic spells

essentials

cassandra eason

foulsham
LONDON • NEW YORK • TORONTO • SYDNEY

foulsham

The Publishing House, Bennetts Close, Cippenham,
Slough, Berkshire, SL1 5AP, England

ISBN 0-572-02827-X

Cover illustration by Jurgen Ziewe

Neither the editors of W. Foulsham & Co. Ltd nor the author nor the
publisher take responsibility for any possible consequences from any
treatment, procedure, test, exercise, action or application of medication or
preparation by any person reading or following the information in this
book. Note, in particular, that some oils, herbs and fragrances are not
suitable for use in pregnancy (see page 4) or for anyone with high blood
pressure or lung or heart problems. Keep a window open if working
indoors with incense or smudge sticks, and keep direct smoke away from
small children and animals. Always take care when using candles. Ensure
that they are secured in a candle holder or similar, do not stand them too
close to curtains or other hanging fabric, and never leave them
unattended.

Printed in Great Britain by Cox & Wyman Ltd, Reading, Berkshire

Contents

Using oils and incenses during pregnancy

Some fragrances are not suitable for use in pregnancy, especially the first three months when you may prefer not to use incense at all. I have included in the list below one or two fragrances not in this book, so that if you come across them you will know to avoid them. This is not a comprehensive list.

The following incense and oils should not be inhaled or taken internally in pregnancy: angelica, anise, basil, bay, caraway, cayenne pepper, fennel, juniper, parsley, poppy, rosemary, sage, thyme, wintergreen and yarrow.

What is Magic?

We all have psychic powers within us that can be used to make our lives happier. One of the easiest and most successful ways of doing this is by using magic. Magic simply means applying the power of thought to bring what would make us happy into our lives and to remove what is making us unhappy.

Scientists have discovered that absolutely everything is made up of moving energy. These energies, of course, are bound up in parcels, such as a car, a specific job or even a person we would like as a lover. In magic we are using our personal energy field to draw to us the parcels of energy we want to make our lives better and to push away from our energy field the parcels of energies that are causing us grief.

Even without the benefit of science, our ancestors knew that what we would call spell-casting could improve their lives. They increased their own powers by drawing on the power sources of natural energies: flowers, trees, herbs, the weather, the Sun and Moon. We too can tap into the same energies to make our spell-casting successful.

What is a spell?

Think of it in terms of cookery. The recipe transforms raw ingredients into the finished product. You start with the aim, for example to make a birthday cake or in magical terms to win a new lover. You get together what you need for the recipe or spell, such as particular candles and crystals, and then you follow a set of stages to attain the end product.

Just as in cooking you need certain conditions, for example an oven at a certain heat for so many minutes, in magic you choose the day and time of day which are most effective for the kind of magic you want to work.

In this magical recipe book there are 80 spells that I know work well in practice. I give you the ingredients, timings and the steps to take. Of course, in time you will want to experiment, like any good cook or magician, and so in each chapter I have listed the most suitable materials and timings, so that you can try out your own formulas and make your own spells.

Making it happen

If it were that simple we would all do spells to become lottery millionaires – and get a pay-out of 5p each when the prize was shared out among all the spell-casters. Magic has its rules that stop us from turning every day into the first day of the cosmic sales with the best spell-casters scrambling to get the best prize.

Magic says that you can ask for enough for your needs and a little more. That means, in essence, that if you desperately need a holiday for your family, you can ask for the sort of holiday you would normally take and not tickets for five in an exclusive resort on a tropical island for a month. People who have exotic holidays have usually made or inherited their money by earthly means and do not necessarily have a better time than I would on a campsite in June with my children.

The power of positive or white magic

Another thing you must always remember is that what you send out in the way of energies comes back three times stronger, so magic must always be used for a positive purpose. Don't use magic if you are angry – dig the garden, go for a walk or clean out a cupboard. Magic should be done in a calm, kind way; don't ask for someone else to be sacked so that you can have his or her job, don't ask for your husband's lover (however deservedly) to fall off a cliff. As a result of positive magic you will find all kinds of good things come into your life unasked, which is why I have included a few spells for helping humanity in general. As for that spiteful lover – she will get what she deserves, in the end.

Following up the spell

Think of spell-casting as creating a huge concentrated amount of energy, like that needed to get a plane off the ground. Like the plane, you need to direct and fuel those energies and have a specific destination or focus. So, after you have tidied away all the material left from your spell, you need to apply that new-found confidence and impetus in a practical way. You need to invite the guy or girl of your dreams for a drink after work, to apply for a new job or to say goodbye to the person who is making you unhappy. The practical steps are the hard ones, but with your magical energy field or aura around you charged up for action, you have a good chance of success. You can always top up flagging energies with more magic followed by more action.

Chapter 1
Beginning Spell-casting

You do not need any special powers to cast successful spells. The magical processes are no different from the intuitive powers that we use every day as a guide. Women are sometimes even called witches because they phone their mother or sister on impulse to ask what is wrong just as that person was dialling their number to tell them of an unexpected crisis. Women, too, wake routinely in the night before a baby cries, even if the infant is in another room. Men do have these powers but tend to trust them less. However, men can be excellent magicians. Look at Merlin.

In a spell, these innate intuitive powers are focused and directed into making things happen in a desired way. Spell-casting is a natural way of taking control of your life and making it closer to what you want.

On pages 11–13 I have listed four simple stages that you can use in creating your own spells, although in practice they tend to be combined. Sometimes, too, if a spell is cast for bringing harmony, the process may be altogether quieter, with soft words and gentle actions. Even the set spells are only examples and you can change them to fit with your own needs and personality because witchcraft is about trusting your own instincts.

What you need to cast spells

Eye of newt and wing of bat are no more relevant to modern magic than a recipe for Sunday lunch that demands you find five young sea urchins from Fiji. For the spells in this book you will already have most of the equipment in the kitchen or garden and the rest you can mainly buy from supermarkets, garden centres and home ware stores. Or you can improvise and adapt with what you happen to have to hand.

Magical tools were traditionally part of home life. The witch's broom with which she swept her magical circle was the same one used for sweeping the yard and was, when not in use, set bristles uppermost against an outside wall to protect the home.

You may already burn oils, incenses and candles in your home, and using them in spells is just an extension of the soothing or energising effects you get when you light a floral incense stick or essential oil to mask the smell of the cat. Lavender works wonders for my beloved but pungent tabby feline Mr Bear.

Essential oils, incenses and crystals are all widely available. Most of the spells in this book use common multi-purpose fragrances and crystals. As well as being potent in spells, crystals can bring positive and protective qualities into your life in the simplest of ways. Try just holding them or soaking them in water and adding the crystalline water to your bath. These powers mean that crystals make lovely birthday and Christmas presents.

Smudge or smoke sticks are used in some of the spells and can be found in New Age and gift stores. I would recommend you buy a mortar and pestle for mixing herbs. These are easily available in most cookware stores, although you can substitute a small bowl and wooden spoon.

How to cast a spell

A spell can be as simple or complicated as you want, but is usually made up of the same four stages. It generally involves repetitive words and phrases, which create a rhythm and build up energies, and actions that tend to be repeated or follow a sequence and also become more intense as the energies increase. However, some spells can rely purely on words or actions. In either case, the ritual serves to focus the energies.

The four stages and the grounding
1 Defining the focus

Why do you want to cast the spell? Once you have decided this you can choose a symbol to act as a focus for the words and actions. Or you could write and then speak the purpose of the spell to focus the energies on a particular aim.

Most of the items that can serve as symbols you will already have: a house key for a moving spell, a model boat or plane from a toy box for a travel spell or a photograph of a person to whom you are sending healing or love.

Whether or not you have an actual symbol, name aloud the intention of the spell and any specific details, such as the time scale within which you need a result or the location to which you want the spell to take you.

2 Starting the action

Next you need to transform your intention or wish into reality by endowing the symbol with life and power. You might begin a chant or start to circle around the symbol. A common method I have used in some of the spells is to pass the symbol through or over the magical substances of the ancient elements: Earth, Air, Fire and Water in turn (see pages 13–14).

Alternatively, you might get the energies circulating by chanting or singing words that express the wish. You may also try a slow spiral dance or play a drum or rattle as you chant.

3 Raising the power

This is the most active and powerful part of the spell, and involves building up the speed and intensity of the action that you started in stage 2.

You could repeat the chant, dance faster or drum with greater intensity until you feel that you have reached a peak of power. This gets the parcel of energy that is your desire moving from the thought plane closer to reality.

4 Releasing the power
At this stage you will release the power into the cosmos by shouting the chant or words such as 'The wish is mine' or 'The power is free'. You might jump or stamp your feet or extinguish a central candle or candles, sending the light to the subject of the spell or to yourself. The flash of released energy should bring the wish into actuality, though you may have to do some earthly work to ensure that this power comes your way.

Grounding the power
To bring yourself back to earth, clear and wash any tools and sit quietly, perhaps playing gentle music or tending plants, making plans for your first practical steps towards fulfilment of the spell.

Using the four elements in magic

The Ancient Egyptians, the Greeks and the Romans all worked with these four elements that were believed to make up all forms of life. They have survived in modern magic, and the magical materials associated with them are all readily available.

Earth

Earth brings stability and ensures the practical success of spells.

Its direction is North.

You can use salt, pot pourri, flower petals, soil or sand as its magical substance. You can scatter a circle of salt or petals around a symbol to give it the power of Earth.

Air

Air gets the energies of the spell moving and can bring swiftness of results to a spell.

Its direction is East.

You can use incense sticks or cones, a smudge stick or feathers to swirl round your symbol and fill it with energy. You could also draw a circle of smoke round the symbol or write in the air with the smoke. The power of Air is particularly strong on a windy day.

Fire

Fire burns through any obstacles to success and adds inspiration and clarity to the spell so that you can see and draw to you the positive outcome.

Its direction is South.

Candles are the most usual form of Fire power. You can pass a symbol through or above the flame to attract the power. A small bonfire can also be used.

Water

Water helps the energies to flow from thought into reality and also ensures that a spell remains positive.

Its direction is West.

You can use still mineral water, water that has been left in Sun or Moonlight, water steeped with rose petals or lavender or rose water.

You could sprinkle a circle of water round the symbol or a few drops on top of it.

Magical correspondences

In each chapter I have listed the best colours, incenses, oils and crystals to use for your own spells. I have repeated this information at the back of the book in table form for easy reference (see pages 184–8). The individual spells include a list of materials that work well, but you can always substitute one from the general list for that topic.

In practice, lavender or rose can be used in place of any other oil or incense. Pine or lemon is good for cleansing and you can use lemon juice if necessary. White candles can be substituted for any colour. An amethyst or rose quartz crystal can be used for any gentle healing or calming spells and a clear quartz crystal for giving energy.

Your usual jars of cooking herbs will be more than adequate for spell-casting and sage is the all-purpose herb. As with cookery, you can instinctively make substitutions for ingredients you do not have. Creativity is the key to good spell-casting.

If you do not have a symbol to represent your need, you can make one out of clay or dough, draw it or write its name on a piece of paper. The magic is within you and the tools are just accessories to the real power source.

When to cast your spells

You can cast a spell whenever you need to. If you want or need something urgently, the sheer intensity of emotion will carry the spell through regardless of the day of the week or the phase of the Moon.

However, if you do have a choice, then at certain times and on particular days, the energies do flow more easily for certain kinds of spells. It is rather like swimming with, rather than against, the tide.

In each chapter, I have listed the most suitable day of the week for each spell. Friday is the best day for love spells, for example, because the planet Venus who was the goddess of Love rules Friday. I have written in more detail about magical times and experiences in my *Practical Witchcraft and Magical Spells* (Quantum 2001), but for practical purposes I have given all the basic information you will need in this book.

Much of the reasoning behind the timing of spells is quite logical, for example, rainy days for washing things away, windy days for blowing positive change into our lives, spells on the turning tide for that moment of power when the sea crashes on the shore and then surges back. A wish made as you cast a stone or shell into the waves is, as any child knows, carrying a whole lot of energy to bring it to fruition. Above all you will sense the time for a particular spell, using the same instincts with which we can feel, on the stirring air, a storm coming to clear away mugginess and stagnation.

The power of the Moon

Under the timing of individual spells I have sometimes listed the appropriate phase of the Moon. The Moon is the special friend of the spell-caster since her changing monthly energies link in well with different needs and the crescent Moon brings a new beginning every month. Except on the day of the full Moon, her energies are gentle and harmonise well with human feelings.

As the Moon's light increases or waxes, so the energies to attract good things and luck also increase. After the night of the full Moon, the energies wane or decrease until you are back where you started at the new Moon. You can use the waning or decreasing energies like a draining bath to carry away what is no longer needed in your life.

On clear nights you can see the phase of the Moon. When the Moon is waxing, the light increases each night from right to left. Then, after the full Moon, the light gradually disappears, also from right to left. The waxing Moon has its light on the right side, the waning Moon on the left.

Your best friend, especially on cloudy nights, is *Old Moore's Almanack*, which will tell you exactly what the Moon and indeed the Sun are doing throughout the year. This can be bought at most newsagents and bookshops. You can also check the weather chapter of your local paper for lunar phases and times of the rising and setting of the Moon.

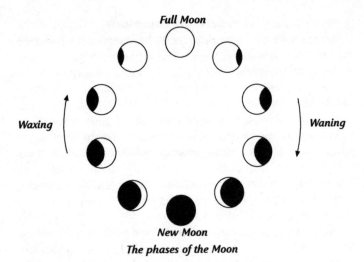

Full Moon

Waxing

Waning

New Moon
The phases of the Moon

Waxing Moon energies

These energies are apparent from when you first see the crescent in the sky to the night before the full Moon. Waxing energies are good for spells to increase success and happiness in your personal and work life, to start and develop ideas and projects, especially money-spinning plans and creative ventures, to learn new skills, to attract a lover, to make new relationships or deepen existing ones.

The night when the crescent Moon is first in the sky is the best for new beginnings. Remember when you turned over your money as a child and bowed three times before making a wish? The three bows represent the three main phases of the Moon as were sacred to the Ancient Egyptian holy family, Osiris the god, Isis the goddess and Horus their son.

Full Moon energies

Though strictly there is only one day of pure full Moon energies, the days on either side are also very powerful.

In your spells, full Moon energies can be used when you need to make a major leap or change in your world, and for speaking what needs to be said, whether that is 'I love, you', 'I am sorry', 'I am no longer afraid of you' or 'Goodbye'.

The full Moon is also a good time for casting spells for becoming pregnant or for launching major creative or business ventures.

Waning Moon energies

The energies of a waning Moon can be used for removing everything that is unwanted in your life and for reducing the power of bad habits or destructive relationships. It is also a good time for spells to finish projects and for reducing debt or losing weight, overcoming nightmares or insomnia, reducing pain and for increasing your psychic powers as the outer world becomes less powerful.

Sun times

As well as Moon energies, you can give your spells a burst of Sun power by working at the four change times of the day. While the Moon operates monthly, the Sun cycle repeats daily. The effect of these energies is more instant and good for short-term, immediate or urgent needs.

Dawn and dusk vary each day by a few minutes.

Dawn

Dawn is the time for new beginnings in any venture, for optimism, for change and gain, whether in love, wealth, health or happiness. It is also the time for gentle healing.

Its direction is East.

Noon

Noon energies can be used when there is a sudden or urgent need for power, action, success, confidence, strength, healing or a fast infusion of money.

Its direction is South.

Dusk

Dusk is a good time for spells to leave behind the tension, guilt, resentment or regret accumulated during the day. It is also the time for protective or domestic magic and for spells involving divination.

Its direction is West.

Midnight

Midnight is the time for spells for forgiveness, for letting go of the past and for healing abuse. It is also the time for spells for older family members and friends.

Its direction is North.

Sun and Moon power together

When the Moon and Sun are in the sky at the same time a combination of energies are present. On the day of the full Moon around sunset you will see the Moon rising in the East as the Sun is setting in the West. This time can be used to balance your inner and outer needs or two different demands. The waxing Moon will be in the sky especially in its earlier stages when it is still light. Check your *Old Moore* or newspaper for the overlap. At the end of the waning phase you may see the previous day's Moon still in the sky at dawn.

The spells

In the following chapters are 80 spells, divided into different areas, such as love, money and home life. Happiness is the theme of them all, for only if we are happy can we spread happiness and so make the world a better and more joyous place.

Chapter 2
Happy Home Spells

Whether it is a room in a shared flat or a haven we have created lovingly over a number of years, the home is central to our happiness. As the world around us speeds up, so our personal sanctuary becomes increasingly precious as a centre of harmony, spiritual renewal and family unity. As external hostility has increased, conventional security devices can be supplemented with modern versions of ancient spells which weave a psychic energy field around our dwelling to make it and us less vulnerable.

Home spell correspondences

Candles: Pink for kindness and to create a peaceful atmosphere; brown for physical and emotional security; grey for casting protective barriers.

Incenses and oils: Freesia, lilac, lavender, lily, rose, sage and strawberry for happiness; chamomile and rosewood for calm; patchouli, pine and lemon for domestic protection.

Crystals: Amethyst for protection against negative earth energies and ghosts; blue lace agate for peace and gentleness; jade and rose quartz for bringing love and healing sorrow; jet, obsidian, brown agate and brown jasper for strong defence of physical boundaries.

Best time: Saturdays are good for home spells.

A spell to create a happy and harmonious home

This is the most important spell in this chapter, and perhaps in the book. It is quite long but, once cast, it will ensure ongoing happiness in your home. The spell works equally well if you live alone.

In the East it is common to have a shrine to the kitchen god, and in ancient Rome *focus* was the Latin name for the family hearth where the family made offerings to the household gods and to the ancestors. Until the advent of central heating, the hearth remained the focal point of family life.

Some homes always seem light, warm and welcoming. The secret is that they exude a tranquillity that makes everyone feel instantly welcome. This is because they possess a repository of gentle harmonious energies that can absorb any jarring external tensions. This spell works by balancing the ancient elements in order to create the right psychic mix in the home.

For general protection, regularly burn rosewood or chamomile oil, or lilac or strawberry incense in the hall to create a barrier of fragrance.

You will need: A pot of flowers or a dish of pot pourri, a chamomile, lilac, patchouli or strawberry incense stick, a pink candle, a broad-based, heat-resistant candle holder, a small dish of lavender or rose water, a red drawstring bag, a coin, a tiny piece of wood, a silver heart or one cut from pink silk, a silk or dried flower, some seeds and a nut.

Best time: In the late afternoon.

The spell

✧ Choose a room where people naturally gather; I call this the heart of the home. Here you are going to create an ongoing source of harmony.

✧ If there is a natural hearth in the room, this is the ideal thing to use. Alternatively you could use a small table or create a magical hearth by standing some stones or bricks on a slab of slate or stone, and positioning this against a wall.

✧ In the hearth or on the table, set a pot of flowers or dish of pot pourri in the North to indicate Earth.

✧ Place a chamomile, lilac, patchouli or strawberry incense stick in a holder in the East for Air, a pink candle for Fire in the South and a small dish of lavender or rose water in the West for the Water element.

✧ In the centre of the hearth, surrounded by these elemental symbols, place the following items together in a red drawstring bag: a coin for prosperity, a tiny piece of wood for warmth, a silver heart or one cut from pink silk for love, a silk or dried flower for health, some seeds for abundant food and a nut for all kinds of fertility.

✧ Light the candle and incense so that the light and fragrance fall on the bag. Either alone or with your family, hold the bag, endow it with wishes for family happiness and health, not forgetting the needs of absent members, and return it to the hearth.

✧ Carry your pot of flowers through the house, saying in each room or corridor:

Bring quietness and stability, peace and tranquillity to all who live in this house.

✧ Carry the lighted incense through the house, saying:

Blow away disunity, worry and anxiety, leaving only harmony to all who live here.

✧ Using a broad-based, heat-resistant holder, take the candle from room to room, saying:

Light the way homeward, chase away shadows from our sanctuary and from all who live here.

✧ Finally sprinkle lavender or rose water in the centre of every room or corridor, saying:

Flow water lovingly, making words gentle and deeds always kindly. May peace abide for those who live in this house.

✧ Leave the candle and the incense to burn down in the hearth and endow their power to the red bag.

✧ Make sure you keep fresh flowers near the bag and once a month, or when the harmony of the home is threatened, light a new pink candle and incense in the hearth and sprinkle the bag with lavender or rose water.

✧ Plant the nut and seeds from the bag and replace them with new ones.

A spell for clearing away negative energies from your home

A house, like any other place, has a psychic energy field around it. This aura is made up not only of energies good and bad from the immediate environment, but of the collective power of the people who have lived there in the past. Certain rooms may seem dark or cold even in summer and you may notice quarrels break out frequently there, cats won't settle and plants wilt.

The reason may be streams of psychic energy underneath the house that have become blocked by physical pollution or too many electricity pylons or phone masts in the area. Land and houses may also hold memories of unhappy events. Cleansing the home is easy and will have a dramatic effect. If you suspect you have a ghost, the following spell will also help him or her to move on peacefully

You will need: A sage smudge or smoke stick or a pine or lemon incense stick, a bowl of sand, and amethyst crystals.

Best time: A bright sunny day, at noon if possible.

The spell

✧ Begin upstairs in the top left room (as you look at the house). Include any lofts. Light your incense or smudge and make waist-high clockwise circles of smoke around the room, starting at the door.

- ✧ Create spirals of smoke all round the window frames, saying:
  Let nothing dark remain within these walls, sadness will not linger to trouble our days or disturb our nights.
- ✧ When you have finished each room, stand in the centre of the room or passageway. Point your incense or smudge to the four directions. Start by pointing to the approximate North and saying:
  May darkness be gone from the North.
- ✧ Then turn through East, South and West, making an archway of smoke up to about shoulder height as you move, and repeating the appropriate words as you point to each direction.
- ✧ When you have finished, open the window and say:
  I welcome the light. May only good, light, life and loveliness remain.
- ✧ If only certain rooms seem problematic, focus on those.
- ✧ When you have cleansed the whole house or the dark spots, extinguish the incense or smudge in a bowl of sand and open the front and back door.
- ✧ Place amethyst crystals inside the house on either side of the front and back door. Wash these regularly in running water.

A spell for keeping your home and possessions safe from harm

In the past, boundaries were often made of hawthorn, partly because it is a sharp physical deterrent but also because of the spiritual power of protection in this magical plant. Nettles are also defensive magically as well as physically.

Bay trees, palms, cactus, myrtle, juniper and rowan trees and the herbs basil, cumin, wild garlic, parsley, rosemary, sage, thyme and vetivert are also traditional protectors. In apartments, tubs of herbs and potted palms form an excellent psychic defence.

You will need: A silver bell, small wind chimes or Tibetan bells and four small protective herbs or plants in separate pots. Use any green plant if you cannot find one from the list above.

Best time: The first night of the waning Moon. If repeated every few months, this spell will supplement more conventional security devices, by lowering the profile of your home and also sending out psychic 'Do not enter' signals.

The spell

✧ Establish both your psychic and physical home boundaries by ringing the bell or chimes along any external walls, moving from left to right as you face in towards the centre of the room. Continue to do this on every floor of your home, treating any shared walls as external walls.

✧ Outside, ring the bell around the boundaries of your garden or front path if you have one and along any fences or boundary walls.

✧ Next place a protective plant or herb at each of the furthest corners of your property. These can either remain in pots for use inside and out, or be planted in the earth next to a fence or wall.

✧ As you ring the bell and set the plants, visualise a barrier of light enclosing your home and its contents.

✧ Visit each of these corners again and enchant your plant guardians by passing your hands palms downwards, the left moving clockwise, the right anticlockwise simultaneously nine times. Make these movments very slowly a few centimetres above or in front of each plant. As you do so, say:
One from theft, two from storm, three from sickness and from harm, four from fire and careless stranger, five from fire and unseen danger, six from malice, seven from pain, eight from flood, nine from rain. Protect. Nine, eight, seven, six, five, four, three, two, one, may this spell last through Moon and Sun. So shall it be, as I count three, two, one. Protect.

✧ If you have any particularly valuable items, whether in financial or personal terms, hide or tape a few coriander seeds in a piece of rolled up cling film in or close to each item.

A spell for selling your home and buying a new one

Moving home is rated as one of the most traumatic events in a person's life, because there are so many variables. However, a spell can help to harmonise the energies so that buying and selling are more likely to come together. Carry out this spell before any major stages in the process. If you are buying a house for the first time you can omit the selling symbols or adapt them towards getting a mortgage or a deposit and paying conveyancing fees.

You will need: A picture of your current house and the one you are buying or of an ideal house you would like to buy. Also a large metal tray, some paper and a pen, frankincense or fern (or pine or lemon if you cannot find them) incense sticks in holders and four yellow or red candles. (I am suggesting different incenses and candle colours from those generally used for domestic magic as buying and selling need especially fast-moving energies.)

Best time: Any time when you can see the Moon during the waxing Moon period. If things are going too slowly, repeat the spell close to dawn on any waxing Moon day.

The spell

✧ On a large metal tray, create a circle of four red or yellow candles in the four main directions. This need only be approximate. Between each candle set the incense in a holder or tall jar.

✧ In the centre, arrange your pictures so that the picture of the new house is face uppermost on top of the picture of the house you are selling.

✧ Write on separate slips of paper, eight stages or obstacles to be overcome between selling your present home and moving into your new one. Stick to the eight most relevant or pressing stages or obstacles.

✧ Place two slips of paper in front of each candle. Start by lighting the candle in the North, while saying:
So do I give power to my intent. Fly free and return fulfilled.

✧ Then use the candle to light the incense stick to the East, while saying:
Make dream reality. Fly free, return to me fulfilled.

✧ Continue until you have released all eight stages or obstacles into the sky and then say:
From (the house you are trying to sell) to (the house you are trying to buy), I thus empower you. (Give the house names, numbers or areas.)

✧ Blow out the candles in rapid succession. Imagine the light from the candles protecting you as you move into your new home.

✧ Keep the pieces of paper in a drawer and as each is achieved or overcome throw it away.

A spell for moving into a new house

When you move out of a house, try to leave a little of your happiness for the new owner, perhaps a favourite pot plant, the first flowers from the garden in a vase or a small ornament in an alcove where it has been for years.

Young Roman women moving from their family home to get married would take with them burning embers from the family hearth as symbols of protection and good fortune. Though this is not practical in the modern world, you can still take a small item connected with the home that you are leaving in order to transfer good fortune to your new home. This might be a favourite small garden plant in a pot, the door knocker or a door handle from your living room. Be sure to replace the item you choose to take before you move.

Even if you have suffered a run of bad luck, find something associated with happier times: a child's doorplate or cuttings from a rose bush you planted on an anniversary. Make this the last item you pack and carry it in your hand luggage. Also bring just one door key from your old home.

This spell involves making a protective jar, a tradition that was followed by people in Europe and Scandinavia for hundreds of years until the beginning of the last century. These jars were called belleramine jars.

You will need: The chosen item from your old home, a red cord, a door key from your old home and a spare one from the new home, salt, dried or fresh rosemary, a few iron nails (used from Celtic times in protective spells against malevolence, both earthly and paranormal) and a little cheap red wine or wine vinegar (the original protective substance, urine, has fortunately been abandoned in modern spells). Also a small stone or dark glass jar with a lid or cork.

Best time: The evening you move into your new home.

The spell

◇ When you reach your new home, place your transferred object in the most appropriate position.

◇ Before the furniture arrives, open all the windows and doors to let the new life in.

◇ At sunset, open the jar and set it on a table. Using the red cord, and making three knots, tie together your old door key and the key to your new home. At the same time say:
   Old and new, past and future, join. May my door be always open to those who come with friendship in their hearts.

◇ Put the keys and cord into the jar.

◇ Put the iron nails into the jar, while saying:
   Against darkness and doubts, phantoms and foes, protect this my home. May my door be closed to those who come with malice in their hearts.

◇ Next sprinkle salt into the jar, for purification, and either some dried or fresh rosemary, while saying:
   Drive away bad memories, leaving only golden days.

◇ Finally add the red wine or wine vinegar.

✧ Shake the bottle and say:
  Keep safe and joyous my home into the years ahead.
  I dedicate this bottle as guardian spirit and protector.
✧ Bury the bottle as near to the front door as you can or keep it
  in a cellar, a basement or a dark corner where it will not be
  disturbed.

A spell for a beautiful garden

Some people naturally have green fingers and can make a
beautiful garden out of a wilderness or a paved area.
Increasingly people are becoming aware of the essences in
nature that can help us to develop areas of natural beauty and
tranquillity even in an urban setting or on the smallest balcony
or paved area.

You will need: Four small jade stones, moss agates or green
glass nuggets (moss agates are especially associated with gardens
and gardening; you could use just one stone if you are doing
your planting in a pot), nine very small clear quartz crystals or
glass nuggets, a glass jug, still mineral water and a selection of
small plants or seedlings in pots. Also a collection of stones
(these will be used to make a cairn, a pile of stones originally
sacred to the Cailleach the ancient Scottish Crone goddess).

Best time: The three days before the full Moon unless you are
planting bulbs, in which case, work on the day after the full
Moon. Carry out the spell just before dark.

The spell

✧ Preparations for this spell need to begin on the day before the spell itself. Start by burying the jade, moss agate or glass nuggets at the corners of a flower bed; or plant the single stone in a large plant pot.

✧ Early in the morning of the day before the spell, place the nine small quartz crystals in the bottom of a glass jug. Fill the jug with mineral water.

✧ On the morning of the spell, position the plants in their pots in a circle.

✧ Scatter a few drops of the empowered life-force water on to each plant, while saying:
Be filled with light and life. Grow tall and strong and beautiful.

✧ You may become aware of a faint green aura or psychic energy field around each plant as you add the water.

✧ When you have watered the circle of plants, dig holes either in the flower bed or in the large pot in which you buried the crystal/s, sprinkling a little of the water into each hole. As you do so, say:
Root deep that you may live long and seed new life.

✧ Place each plant into a hole, cover the roots with soil and say:
Breathe your green life to purify and beautify the world.

✧ Build a cairn close to the plants by piling the stones on top of one another. If working indoors, place one stone each day

for a week and then one stone once a week. Make a wish for the growth of the garden as you place each stone.
✧ Add the rest of the light water, a few drops at a time to your watering can, and use this to water the flower bed or pot.

A springtime and de-clutter spell

Our distant ancestors used to welcome spring by throwing away the old rushes from the floor and putting on newly washed clothes. In the 1950s the annual spring clean was still a major event and I can remember hauling all the furniture out into the back yard on the first fine spring day. We then scrubbed the house clean, beat the carpets and washed all the bedding or hung it on the washing line to air. At New Year too, especially in Scotland, juniper berries were burned to purify the home. With modern cleaning equipment and air fresheners, spring cleaning is no longer a major event in people's lives.

The psychic energies represented by these physical activities are still important, however, as a way of clearing out stagnant energies and emotional clutter we may have accumulated in family life. On pages 26–7 I suggested a spell for clearing away negative energies. Spring cleaning spells are much lighter and tend to bring fresh psychic air that can renew enthusiasm and lift depression. It is also a good way of getting rid of any redundant attitudes or irritations.

You will need: A big cardboard box, some dried lavender or rose pot pourri and a broom or a wide-nozzle vacuum cleaner.

Best time: The first sunny day around the Spring Equinox (around 21 March in the Northern hemisphere, 21 September in the Southern hemisphere) or any time you feel hemmed in by family clutter.

The spell

✦ Into the cardboard box throw all those unwanted things that have been lying around for months, such as trainers with holes in, socks that don't match and never will, and advertisements for products you will never buy.

✦ When the box is almost full, close the lid or tape up the top and walk round it nine times anticlockwise, saying:
   Clutter and mutter, stagnant and old, clearing be done, as I count down to one. Four, three, two, one, clutter be gone.

✦ Put the box out for the garbage men.

✦ Scatter lavender or rose pot pourri near the front and back doors of your home. Either sweep it out of the door or vacuum it up in anticlockwise circles, saying over and over again:
   Dust to dust, away you must. New life bring, welcome spring.

✦ Spend some time clearing away more physical clutter and then go for a walk in the sunshine.

A spell for renovating and redecorating your home

Building and decorating work can be incredibly fraught, whether you need major renovations involving a team of builders, you are imprinting your personal style on your first home or you are redecorating the odd room. It is a time when we are more likely to suffer minor accidents, not only because of the dangers involved in using tools and climbing up ladders, but because our protective psychic radar can get distracted by the physical disruption. The presence or all too frequent absence of builders, can also lead to headaches and increased stress levels. This spell can help to enhance creativity while also creating calm and positive vibes so that the work becomes a pleasure or at least bearable, rather than a battle zone. See also pages 148–9 for a spell for improving practical skills such as DIY.

You will need: Chamomile or rosewood oil or lilac, strawberry or rose incense. Also five or six small grey candles and a small hand mirror.

Best time: The night before the work begins. If possible, don't decorate during the waning Moon when we are naturally more irritable and accident-prone. Start this spell and the work near the beginning of the Moon cycle for a less hyperactive and more creative initial approach.

The spell

♦ On the night before you start moving furniture, sit in the first room or area to be redecorated or renovated and burn a very gentle chamomile or rosewood oil or some lilac, strawberry or rose incense.

♦ Position a circle of small grey candles on a table in the centre of the room. Light the candles.

♦ Using a small mirror, shine the beams of the candles over the walls and on to the ceiling, saying:
Nought harm, peace, calm. We will make new from old.
Silver beams protection hold.

♦ Extinguish the candles and oil or incense and sit in the darkness, breathing in the lingering fragrance.

♦ Before the walls are redecorated, in age-old tradition, write your family name in a colour that can be covered over.

♦ Alternatively, if furniture is being assembled, scratch your family name underneath one of the drawers or inside one of the legs to bring good fortune to the redecorated room.

Chapter 3

Spells for Personal Happiness, Health and Fulfilment

This is the chapter that can easily be overlooked in spell books. It might seem selfish to do spells purely for yourself, but once you are happy, healthy and fulfilled you are then in a position to enjoy life and relationships fully. These personal happiness spells can help you to fulfil your destiny in your own unique way, to value yourself for what you are, without constantly seeking approval or trying to be what other people want you to be.

A number of happiness and health spells use wind and water, the two forces believed in Oriental spirituality to carry the life force most powerfully.

Happiness spell correspondences

Candles: Orange for a clear identity and self-confidence; yellow for joy and fulfilment; green for self-love; pink for healing, especially of the spirit.

Incenses and oils: Eucalyptus, juniper, mint, sage and tea tree for health and vitality; rosemary and thyme for happiness and harmony; rose and ylang ylang for self-love.

Crystals: Amber and carnelian for self-confidence; boji stones and clear quartz crystals for the life force; jade and sugilite for harmony and gentle energy; kunzite and rose quartz for self-love and healing of sorrow.

Best time: Sundays are best for health and happiness spells.

A spell for good health

Of all the spells I am asked for, those for restoring and maintaining good health are among the most popular. Even wealth and worldly success cannot compensate for chronic illness or crippling depression. This spell works by attracting and maintaining health-giving energies around you.

An ancient Celtic ritual involved finding nine quartz crystals in a running stream, boiling the crystals in water taken from the stream, allowing the water to cool and then drinking it over nine days to restore vitality and ensure continuing good health. In the modern world few streams would be sufficiently unpolluted to drink the water even after boiling, but the principle of this spell remains the same. Quartz crystals can be used to give energy to people, places, animals and plants (they were used in the gardening spell to make empowered water).

You will need: Seven pieces of fruit (these need only be small and can be of the same kind, for example grapes or plums), a white cloth, a clear glass or crystal bowl, 1 litre/1¾ pints of still mineral water and nine very small clear quartz crystals (you can substitute clear glass nuggets). Also small glass bottles.

Best time: From dawn till noon.

The spell
◇ At daybreak, set your nine quartz crystals in the bowl and fill it with the mineral water.
◇ Leave the bowl where it will be empowered with natural light until noon.
◇ At noon, on the white cloth set your seven pieces of fruit, one for each day of the week.
◇ Sprinkle each fruit in turn with the light- and crystal-infused water, saying:
   You days of the week, with health overflow, with life and with healing, may your radiance show.
◇ Eat the seven pieces of fruit (you can just cut a piece of each if they are large), saying:
   I take in your healing and your strength and thank you for the blessings of health.
◇ If there are any areas of your body or life, physical or emotional, that need healing, you can name them before you eat a fruit.
◇ Use any remaining fruit in a fruit salad.
◇ Pour the remaining water into the small glass bottles. This water can be used over the coming days to add to baths or drinks or to splash on your pulse points when you feel tired.

✧ Keep the crystals where they can absorb natural light every day and if you feel exhausted or unwell, press one of them on the place of pain or tension or in the centre of your hairline for general energy (see also the spell on pages 46–8 for boosting your energy levels).

✧ Wash the crystal in a little of the empowered water after use.

✧ It can be helpful to make a regular supply of light- and crystal-infused water for when you need a quick lift.

A spell for healing sorrow and abuse from the past

Happiness can depend not only on what is happening in the external world but also on what we carry in our minds. Positive messages from parents, teachers, former lovers, employers and friends can encourage us to believe in ourselves and to ask for what we need from others and from life. However, if we have been treated unkindly or coldly in the past, whether physically or emotionally, it can be hard to shake off the old messages. We may not believe we are worthy of love and respect and this can lead to problems in later relationships. This is a spell that can be repeated whenever you doubt yourself.

You will need: A small branch or plant with dead leaves, a vase or holder for the branch or plant, lengths of dark thread long enough to make a knot in, a small evergreen branch or plant and orange, yellow, green and pink ribbons.

Best time: Any windy day.

The spell

✧ Set the branch with dead leaves in the vase or holder.

✧ Take a dark thread to represent a sorrow, name the sorrow aloud and tie the thread loosely to a leaf, saying:
It is gone, it is done. Peace come.

✧ Continue tying threads and naming sorrows until you feel at peace. It does not matter how many or how few unhappy things you recall.

✧ After you have tied each thread, say:
It is gone, it is done. Peace come.

✧ Take the branch out of the vase, take it to a windy place, a hilltop, an exposed beach or an open area of parkland and stand it in the earth. If you have time, watch the leaves blow away. If not, walk off without turning back.

✧ When you get home, set your evergreen branch or plant in the same vase or holder, but this time fill the vase with water.

✧ Tie your coloured ribbons to the evergreen branch, naming for each ribbon a present joy, blessing or success, however small. You can tie more than one ribbon of the same colour. Notice how much more confident you now feel.

✧ Whenever you pass the evergreen branch, touch one of the ribbons and send love to yourself. When the branch dies, it will have served its purpose.

A spell for increasing self-love and self-esteem

In some spell books you may find rituals to make you more beautiful, often involving empowering some aromatherapy products. Apart from the beneficial physical effects of rose water, for example, on your skin, the most important factor is that you feel more beautiful and so radiate beauty.

I am not sure that the emphasis on becoming lovelier in the world's terms either through physical or magical means is as valuable as increasing inner radiance. Sometimes even physically attractive women can give off ugly vibes because they are worried about their appearance, whereas others, who may have physical blemishes or imperfections, are in fact charismatic and attractive.

If you feel confident about yourself and love yourself, which is very different from being obsessed about your looks, then people will comment how young and well you are looking and ask if you have a new hairdo or have lost weight.

You will need: A swimming pool or a safe natural water pool either with sunlight reflecting in it or artificial lights shining on the water. Obviously sunlight is better. You do not need to be a good swimmer as the spell can be carried out in the shallows where you can stand up. In an emergency you can adapt the spell for a bath or Jacuzzi.

Best time: Whenever you can find a quiet time.

The spell

✧ Stand first where there is no light reflected on the water and make anticlockwise circles with your arms. Push away the water all round you, saying in your mind:
  Doubts and dullness, flow from me, lost in darkness may you be.

✧ Now swim, float or walk to a circle of light reflected in the water and make rippling circles all round yourself with your arms.

✧ Swirl the water in clockwise circles, saying in your mind:
  Light and loveliness, enter me, radiate on all I see. Lovely am I and lovely I will be.

✧ Continue moving from individual light pool to light pool, repeating the words and movement until you feel glowing with light.

A spell for boosting energy levels

Untying knots has traditionally been a way of releasing energy. Up until the sixteenth century in Europe and Scandinavia, witches would sell knotted cords to sailors. These knots were thought to have the power to release winds when they were untied. Indeed when the King of Sweden was fighting the Danes in 1563, he took four witches to sea with him to manipulate the weather in his favour.

In the same way, you can symbolically store up energy for when you need a sudden boost or have a series of long days and late nights ahead and cannot catch up on sleep.

You will need: An undyed cord small enough to carry with you, but long enough to take three knots.

Best time: A windy morning. The day of the full Moon is ideal but any day during the waxing period will do.

The spell

✧ Tie one end of your cord firmly to a tree or the outside of a window. The cord should be positioned at your own head level. Leave it for an hour. (If there is no wind, you can hold the cord in front of an electric fan for a few minutes before hanging it outside.)

✧ At the end of the hour, untie the cord and hold it at both ends so that it is taut in front of your face.

✧ Blow three times slowly and gently along the cord, imagining with each breath the sails of a boat filling with air and billowing.

✧ Tie the first knot at the right hand end of the cord saying:
May the four winds enter this knot and hold the power within.

✧ Tie a knot in the middle and then at the other end, repeating the words.

✧ Finally blow three more times over the knotted cord, but more forcefully than before and then say:
Knot of three, till you are free, hold tight your power, until the hour I call thee.

47

✧ When you need a sudden increase in energy, untie one of the knots and say in your mind:
   One knot of three, the power's in me. So shall be free vitality.
✧ Untie the other two knots when necessary, repeating the chant, but modifying it to
   Two knots of three
   and finally
   Three knots of three.
✧ When you have used all three knots of energy, bury or burn the cord.

A de-stressing spell

If you have ever watched a dog shaking itself after coming in from the rain, you will understand the release of tension such an action can bring. If we are really stressed, then even a bath can sometimes leave us still feeling vaguely edgy, because the water is not continuously moving. For stress that has built up over a period, a rainstorm is a good focus, but for instant results use a shower, a Jacuzzi or a waterfall in a fun pool at a leisure centre.

You will need: Any continuously moving, powerful water source in which you can immerse yourself.

Best time: Rainy days or evenings or whenever you feel stressed or overwhelmed by worries or burdens.

The spell

✧ If you are using a shower, turn it on before entering the shower cubicle and use tepid rather than warm water. Leave your shoes outside the bathroom. Throw all your clothes in the wash basket.

✧ If it is a wet day, run out into the rain, wearing a light cagoule or rain mac if you wish, but leaving at least your hair uncovered.

✧ In either case, shake your head, your hands and arms, your feet and legs and whole body, repeating over and over:
Waterfall take stress from me, leave me free, in harmony.

✧ Visualise dark water pouring from you and flowing away.

✧ When you feel liberated, turn off the water source or come indoors and shake yourself like a dog, while repeating the chant.

✧ Dry yourself thoroughly and put on fresh, loose clothes. If it is evening, go to bed early or if morning, spend just a minute or two away from the chaos, breathing in and out very gently, visualising a waterfall flowing over you in your mind.

✧ You can recall your waterfall and the physical sensation of the water at stress points during the coming days.

A spell for establishing your separate identity

There are a number of reasons why we suddenly need to affirm our separate identity. We may find ourselves alone after a relationship break up or when our children leave home. We may move away from friends and family to start college or a job in another part of the world or quit a firm after a number of years either because of retirement or redundancy or for a career change or improvement.

Even if the change is a happy one, it can be hard if we have been bound up with people for a number of years to function as a separate individual away from familiar office gossip and socialising or getting teenagers up for school each morning. Mothers especially can have spent many years worrying about and looking after their children; their departure can leave a huge hole in our lives. It is all too easy, no matter how successful we are career wise, to assume the persona of Mum, as I have within my family, to the exclusion of almost everything else. As I write this, two of my children, whom only yesterday, it seems, I was taking to play school in a double pushchair, have gone off together to the pub, leaving me with the cats and a snack supper for one.

Above all, if a partner walks out or you divorce, half of yourself seems to have gone (see also pages 103–4) even if the relationship was awful.

You will need: A computer is a useful tool for redrawing your boundaries, but you can as easily use a notebook and pen. Also a vase of flowers or a green plant in a pot.

Best time: During the afternoon on any waxing Moon day. You may see the Moon pale in the sky.

The spell

✧ Draw an image of yourself and the person or people with whom your life is or was most recently entwined. A key person can be used to represent a firm. Either use the first page of a notebook or your computer screen and a simple drawing programme or even a digital camera image.

✧ Draw the images so that they touch.

✧ Now alter the picture or draw a second picture on a fresh piece of paper in the notebook so that you and the other person are slightly further apart. Begin to emphasise your own outline around the head. Begin also to draw around the outline of the other person's head.

✧ Continue drawing the figures further apart and highlighting more of the two outlines each time until you have two separate and emphasised outlines.

✧ For children or beloved friends, as you make the final separate outlines on the same piece of paper, say in your own words that the love remains and that they are always in your heart. You could say something like:

Be happy until we meet again.

✧ If the person to whom you were emotionally joined was destructive or made you unhappy or you left the firm unwillingly or with coercion, remove their image from the screen or draw yourself alone on a separate piece of paper.

✧ As you exclude the other person, say:

Go in peace.

In this way you can claim back your self image without tearing it with bitterness in the parting.

✧ Save the final image. You can throw away any other drawings. If you used a computer, print out the final picture.

✧ Stick the picture on your bedroom mirror where you can see it and keep a vase of flowers or a green plant beneath it. If you have separated from children, family or friends, whenever you water the plant or change the flowers you can send words of love to their image. The separateness will not in any way diminish the affection you share, but will allow you to move forward to a new stage in your life.

A spell for finding true happiness

This is an important spell connected with all those dreams you may have held unfulfilled for years or which are emerging in your life. Even within the happiest relationships there is part of ourselves we need to fulfil, the unique destiny we all possess.

The spell is best carried out when there is a rainbow in the sky, so keep the materials to hand at home so you can rush outside when the rainbow appears. Once you have carried out the spell you can repeat the words and visualise the actions wherever you are when the rainbow appears. If you are urgently in need of the spell, use a multi-coloured fibre optic lamp in a darkened room or rainbow Perspex on a window in sunlight to create an instant rainbow.

You will need: A long sheet of strong white paper, small pots of the seven rainbow paints, red, orange, yellow, green, blue, indigo and violet, seven small brushes and a pure white pebble.

Best time: When you see a rainbow.

The spell

♦ Stand outdoors where you can see the rainbow in the sky.
♦ Focus on the colours and say:
  Rainbow, rainbow, magic measure, on your path I wend.
  Show me, magic rainbow, what gift lies at the end.
♦ On your long strip of paper, paint very fast the seven colours in ascending order, chanting over and over:
  Rainbow power, enter here, the gift you bring now show me clear. Red action, orange independence, yellow joy, green love, blue career, indigo knowledge, violet healing.
♦ Try to finish painting while the rainbow remains in the sky.
♦ While you are waiting for the paint to dry, repeat the colours and think about what each gift means in terms of fulfilling your dreams.
♦ When the paint is dry, cast your pebble on the paper rainbow to see which gift this particular rainbow brings, repeating:
  Rainbow, rainbow, magic measure, on your path I wend.
  Show me, magic rainbow, what gift lies at the end.
♦ Where your pebble lands will indicate your way forward. The answer may be a surprise.

✧ Finally swirl round clockwise seven times, saying:
   Rainbow magic, bring to me, what it is that now I see.
✧ Close your eyes, open them and you will have a vision
   externally or in your mind's eye as to how you can take the
   first steps to fulfilment.

A spell for peaceful sleep and for overcoming insomnia

When I was young, bedtime was a transition period of cocoa
and quiet talk by the fire. Now we tend to watch television in
bed before sleep. I sometimes switch off the computer after an
evening's work, have a quick bath and then lie awake with my
body exhausted but my mind whirring. Especially if you have
children, preparations for the morning can mean we are doing
chores until late at night. The following spell is especially good
for busy people, but is also a good way of soothing an insomniac
child.

In this spell you gradually substitute inner for outer light.

You will need: A large pink rose quartz unpolished crystal or
an unpolished pale purple piece of amethyst. Calcite in any of
its shades is also good. These are widely available and very
inexpensive. Also three small pink rose or lavender scented
candles or nightlights. The fragrance will encourage you to rest.

Best time: Any night before sleep.

The spell

✧ On a table facing your bed, light the three scented candles and set them in a horseshoe shape behind the crystal.

✧ Sit in bed and focus on the crystal and the light.

✧ Through half-closed eyes, picture the crystalline light expanding so that it fills the whole room.

✧ Extinguish one of the outer candles, saying:
Light surround, protect, enfold me while I sleep.

✧ Hold in your mind the image of the crystal light enfolding you and enclosing the whole room as brightly as before, though one physical light source has gone.

✧ Extinguish the other outer candle. Repeat the words, still holding the image of encircling light in your mind even after the second physical light source is extinguished.

✧ Extinguish the final candle and as you say the words, picture the light in your mind as though it was still present externally.

✧ Lie down and close your eyes, floating on cotton wool clouds.

✧ Hold the light in your mind until you fall asleep.

✧ In the morning wash the crystal under running water and return it to the table with fresh candles for whenever you need to repeat the spell.

Chapter 4
Relationship Spells

In the chapter on love I suggest spells for happy love relationships, but there are a lot of other people with whom we share our lives and whose actions and words have influence over our emotional well being. Most of us have idealised views of how family life should be. I was very impressed before having my own children by an American television series of a large, poor but happy country-dwelling family called the Waltons. They cheerfully shared chores and created heart-warming meals with the contents of the vegetable patch with not a whinge or a food fad this side of the Rockies. The reality of my own Walton clan is closer to that other great American television family, the Simpsons. In fact I have just had to stop writing to unblock the sink, as water flowed merrily over the kitchen floor while my son cooked bacon blissfully unaware of the rising tide around his ankles.

Nevertheless, the family can be our greatest strength and so this chapter concentrates on spells to reinforce those links. These bonds are ever more complex as many of us add to our families through remarriage or new permanent relationships. This means we can end up with several sets of in-laws and step relations with whom we are suddenly cast into close proximity.

I have included a spell for family occasions such as christenings and weddings in the chapter on social spells.

Relationship spell correspondences

Candles: Pink for gentle love, children, younger relations, harmony and forgiveness; brown for all domestic and practical issues and older family members; silver for mothers and grandmothers; gold for fathers and grandfathers.

Incenses and oils: Chamomile for gentleness and children; lavender for love and kindness; lilac and mimosa for all family matters; orange and sage for a secure family basis; rose for reconciliation and affection; rosewood for domestic harmony.

Crystals: Amber and amethyst and all brown stones, including banded agates, for stability; blue lace agate for softening criticism; all jaspers and fossilised wood for general family matters; jade for children and peace at home; kunzite for adolescents; moonstones for women and mothers; obsidian for older people; rose quartz for children and healing,

Best time: Friday is the best day for relationship and family spells.

A spell for a happy family

Whether you are a household of two, a single parent or a unit of many different generations, a happy family is a source of strength and offers a sense of security and a chance to be truly ourselves. It is the unit of love that we can draw on or withdraw into when the world gives us a hard time.

On pages 23–5 you will find a spell for a happy home and on pages 162–4 a spell for a happy holiday. This spell is for the people who make up the family, whether together, at home, on holiday or apart in different places.

You will need: A large sage smudge stick or sage or orange incense stick and a circle large enough to hold photographs of the family. You can use a child's hoop or create one from stones, glass nuggets and pebbles, large flowers or shells. Also photographs of all the family members.

Best time: Any time, but it can be particularly useful when a member of the family needs support or when a major family change is about to take place.

The spell

◇ Make your circle on a small table and set the photographs within the circle so there are spaces between them. Work in the heart of the house where people congregate or on the ground outdoors if it is sunny.

◇ Light your smudge or incense stick and join the photographs by making smoke spirals in the air just above the pictures. As you do this, softly repeat over and over again:
   Bind invisibly in love my family, that whether near or far from home, we are united still in love and harmony.

◇ Just above the circle itself make smoke knots at approximately the four main directions, North, East, South and West, saying for each:

I make this knot in the North/East/South/West, to secure the unseen love between us all. Blessings be on this family of mine.

✧ Leave the incense or smudge stick to burn down in a safe place.

✧ You may like to find a place in the heart of the house where you can display the photos with a vase or pot of flowers or greenery.

A spell for resolving family quarrels

A family quarrel can occasionally become set in stone long after the original cause has been forgotten and can even be carried on by members of the next generation.

The expression 'burying the bone' comes from the idea of laying to rest old grievances. This ritual involved engraving a word or name, summing up the quarrel, on an animal bone and then burying the bone in a very deep hole at night. In the modern world, it may be easier to use melting candle wax to allow the old dead grudges to flow away and sometimes to bring reconciliation in an unexpected way.

You will need: A small, dark-coloured wax candle, a sharp nail or penknife to engrave it, a flat holder or metal tray. Use a fast-burning candle (some candles say on the label the number of hours they will burn for).

Best time: Any time during the waning Moon period after twilight.

The spell

◇ On the side of the candle, before lighting it, etch a symbol or a word to represent the core issue of the quarrel or coldness. Take your time and as you scratch the wax, feel any resentment against the person leaving you and entering the wax.

◇ Light the candle and, gazing into the flame, voice for the last time what it is that keeps you apart from the family member. As you speak, you may feel your attitude softening, even if the person has been very unkind or unjust.

◇ When you are finished, blow out the candle, saying:
Light of kindness, carry only good feelings and gentle words from me to (name of person), to bring peace if it is right to be.

◇ Relight the candle and this time stand, in your mind, in the shoes of the other person and speak on their behalf. Offer what mitigation you can for their behaviour or try to give their understanding of the situation that caused the rift.

◇ When you have finished, blow out the candle again, saying once more:
Light of kindness, carry only good feelings and gentle words from (name of person) to me, to bring peace if it is right to be.

◇ Light the candle for the third time and say:
Burn away the pain, melt the coldness round my heart and yours, and let there be peace between us/within the family.

◇ While the candle burns through, write a letter of reconciliation or, if this is not appropriate, devise a way of easing tension within the family.

✧ When the candle has burned down, collect any remaining wax and bury it deep in the ground.

✧ If practical, send your letter or make some gesture of peace, if only for your own sake.

A spell for getting on well with in-laws and step relations

Both in-law and step relationships can be hazardous, especially at first since you are suddenly thrust into close proximity, emotionally and physically, with people who are virtual strangers and who may have very different lifestyles from your own. With step relationships especially, you can find yourself being compared with your predecessor who may suddenly acquire the virtues of an Archangel. The key is to meet on an area of common ground. This spell will help you to merge more easily into what may feel like alien territory.

You will need: Two small hoops or circles made out of wire or pliant cane (the kind that straw baskets are woven round) and modelling clay or dough. Also a brown ribbon for each of the people in the new step/in-law relationship (include new sisters- and brothers-in-law, their children plus any new step or grandparents-in-law). Make the ribbons for you and your partner very long. Also a fabric bag to hold all the clay or dough figures and ribbons.

Best time: Any time before the first official get-together, before noon if possible.

The spell

◇ Arrange the two hoops so that there is an overlapping area between them. Make the overlap quite large.

◇ Use the clay or dough to mould tiny figures to represent each member of the two families to be joined, beginning with yourself and the person connecting you with the new family, usually your partner. However, the link can be a grown up child who is marrying into a new family or acquiring stepchildren. The figures do not need features, but mark each with an initial to identify them.

◇ Place yourself and your partner or the person linking you to the other family in the overlapping part of the two hoops.

◇ Set the other figures in their respective family circles.

◇ First you need to make sure of your connection with your partner to avoid anyone else pulling you apart emotionally.

◇ Gently bind these two figures together with your own and your partner's ribbons and tie with three knots, making sure you leave plenty of ribbon spare. As you do this, say:
Three times the lover's knot secure, firm be the knot, long the love endure.

◇ Now, beginning with the other family, take one of the figures and set it in the overlapping circle. Loop a ribbon with a triple knot round the figure and attach it to yours and your partner's entwined ribbons with three more knots, saying:
Three times the knot with love secure, firm be the bond, long the bond endure.

✧ Then attach one of your own family in the same way, repeating the chant.
✧ Continue until all the figures are in the overlap of the hoops, in a heap, joined together with ribbon.
✧ Remove the hoops and put the clay or dough figures in the fabric bag. Take this bag to the get-together and keep it hidden somewhere nearby.
✧ When the figures crumble, you can dispose of them, but tie all the ribbons together in a long cord and keep it behind a door in your home.

A spell for coping with difficult relations

The visit of critical relations can fill us with dread, especially if this is a regular occurrence. If the relation is elderly or close family it may not be possible to confront them or stop the visits. A spell before the visit can, however, help to soften the atmosphere and create an aura or a psychic energy field of gentleness throughout the home that is hard to penetrate even with a sharp tongue. You can also prepare the main room in which the family member generally sits by removing all mirrors and sharp or pointed objects and leaving tiny bowls of rose or lavender pot pourri around the room. You may also like to burn chamomile essential oil.

You will need: Four very small blue lace agate or jade crystals (these have the power to soften words), a large bottle of still mineral water, a jug or bowl and a blue cloth or scarf.

Best time: Whenever needed. Grey or misty days are especially good.

The spell

✧ About six hours before the visit, gently drop your four blue lace agates into the bottle of mineral water, saying:
Be still, harsh tongue, be silent, unkind words, fade away, bitter thoughts and leave only love and gentleness.

✧ Put on the lid and cover the bottle with a blue cloth or scarf, saying:
Sleep softly, slumber deep and bring kindness and tranquillity.

✧ Just before the visit, take out the crystals and set them in the four corners of the room.

✧ Pour a little of the water into a bowl or jug and sprinkle it around the room, saying:
Water of gentleness, bring tenderness.

✧ The rest of the water should be given to the visitor. You might put it in their tea, coffee or juice, or use it to cook the vegetables if they are staying for a meal.

A spell for coping with family troubles

Sometimes it can be a general family problem that is causing anxiety among family members. This might involve financial difficulties, troubles with housing or neighbours (see also the spell on pages 87–8).

One of the worst aspects of being a parent is watching a beloved child, even in the form of a taciturn teenager, having problems at school or socially and feeling helpless to do anything. Many years ago it was the custom for a mother to throw earth or soil after her departing child, to offer him or her the protection of Mother Earth while away from home. I still do this very subtly if I know one of my children is under pressure.

Whether you are focusing on children's or another family member's troubles, bubble blowing is a good way of dissipating worry or sorrow that can create a psychic cloud over family life. If a child is quite young, he or she may enjoy blowing the problems away with you.

You will need: A children's bottle of bubbles with blower or you can use a bowl of very soapy water and some wire twisted into a small circle and a handle, and a packet of seeds.

Best time: Any clear morning in a flat open place where the bubbles can easily fly away.

The spell

✧ Go to an open space and look directly upwards at a clear patch of sky.

✧ Shake the bottle of bubbles nine times and say:
Above, below and all around, from highest sky to lowest ground, so I blow these troubles away.

✧ Slowly blow your first bubble and, as it ascends, name the first or main problem, adding:
Fly high to the sky, no more to stay, so I blow these troubles away.

✧ Blow as many bubbles as you wish for each aspect of the problem or other difficulties that are causing family unhappiness. Repeat for each:
Fly high to the sky, no more to stay, so I blow these troubles away.

✧ When you have finished, walk away, scattering seeds behind you without looking back.

A spell for healing and helping frail older relations

In more traditional societies, the elderly and sick were part of the extended family. But with families living in smaller units, women working and people living much longer, there can be problems in making sure older members of the family are cared for, especially with the decline in help from the State. As well as actual contact when possible, and letters and phone calls when it is not, you can cast a healing or uplifting spell to an older family member or indeed anyone in the family who is unwell and away from home.

You will need: A white or pink cloth and a pale brown or beeswax candle (beeswax is lovely and is associated with St Anne the grandmother of Christ and with older people generally). A bowl, dried rose petals, lavender heads or dried chamomile flowers plus dried cooking sage (alternatively use a fragrant pot pourri based on rose and lavender). Also rose or lavender essential oil, a wooden spoon and a small, cloth purse or drawstring bag that you can buy or make.

Best time: Whenever needed after dusk, 10pm is an hour especially associated with healing, perhaps because before the invention of gas and electric light this was generally a dark, quiet time.

The spell
✧ On a small table, put a white or pink cloth and light a beeswax or pale brown candle.
✧ Add the dried flowers or pot pourri and sage to the bowl and pour in a few drops of essential oil, while softly speaking the name of the person to whom healing is to be sent:
   I wish to send healing to (name of person) who is in (place where person lives).
✧ This is a good way of focusing the healing energies directly on the person in need.
✧ Next look into the candle flame, visualising the face of the person and recalling their voice, and send a few private words of healing.

✧ With the spoon begin to stir the flowers, herbs and oil, chanting very softly but faster and faster:
Flowers of healing, oil of light, love revealing, send your healing, with this light.

✧ When you can feel the flowers and herbs are filled with your love and the healing power of the oil and the light from the candle, stop mixing.

✧ Leave the flowers and herbs in the bowl in the candlelight while you write a note or wrap a few small items to send in a parcel to your relation.

✧ When the candle is burned down, scoop the flowers and herbs into the purse or drawstring bag and add it to the note or gifts you are sending.

A spell for happy family gatherings

Family gatherings at Christmas, weddings, birthdays or christenings are a good way of catching up with family news and coming together in pleasurable way. On pages 85–7 I have suggested a spell for some of these landmark times.

This spell is more general, based on the theory that when you have a number of people in close proximity in a confined space, perhaps eating unusually rich food, all of whom know the weak spots and trigger points of the others, there can be tensions and rivalries even in the most loving families. This spell keeps the happy occasion and underlying good will to the forefront of everyone's minds.

This spell uses flower essences, which are readily available in chemists and health food shops. The essences are natural harmonisers and can also be added to water to spray or sprinkle round the room before a family gathering. My personal favourite family gathering essences are Dr Bach's Red Chestnut or Cerrato, the five flower Rescue Remedy, Chestnut Bud or Water Violet.

You will need: A pink or white cloth, fronds of greenery from a number of different plants, ferns or trees, a vase or pot to hold the fronds, your favourite flower essence or rose or lavender water.

Best time: The day before the family gathering, around twilight. The days just before the full Moon are especially powerful for increasing unity. You can precede the spell by gathering the greenery during the afternoon, if possible with other family members.

The spell
✧ Spread a pink or white cloth on a table and in the centre set the vase, partly filled with water.
✧ Take a frond of greenery for each of the members of the family. Name each person and say:
You are welcome.
✧ Sprinkle a few drops of flower essence or lavender or rose water over each frond in turn, saying:
Kindly be and filled with understanding.

69

✧ When you have blessed each piece of greenery, add them one by one to the vase, saying for each:
Mix and join, blend and harmonise this family, in unity and love.

✧ Place the vase of greenery near the centre of the main room in which the family will be gathering.

A spell for saying bon voyage or goodbye to a family member

If a family member is going away overseas or to live at the other end of the country or is moving in with someone that will make it more difficult to see them regularly, you can carry out this spell to ensure the link of love remains.

I have also known people who have carried out this ritual after the funeral of a loved family member as a private leave-taking or if they were unable to attend the ceremony. Spells are not just about asking for things. Sometimes they can be cast to send love or to mark a personal moment of significance.

You will need: A symbol or photograph of the subject of the spell, paper and a pen, white ribbon, dried rose petals or rose pot pourri and a small box to hold the symbol or photograph.

Best time: I like the Celtic idea of farewell rituals taking place in the early morning, so heralding a renewal of life.

The spell
✧ If possible, work outdoors on a large flat-topped stone, a tree stump or a picnic table.

✧ If this is not possible, find a place in the house from which you can see the rising Sun or that faces approximately East.

✧ Set all the materials for the ritual on the flat surface. Stand in front of the stone so that you are facing the direction of the rising Sun.

✧ Hold the photograph or symbol in the air between your hands and offer it to the East, saying:
  Though I may no longer share the days with you, yet will my love be constantly renewed with the morning light. May peace go with you on your journey.

✧ Scatter a circle of rose petals or pot pourri round the symbol, saying:
  Though I may no longer hear your voice each day, yet will your memory be renewed with each rising Sun.

✧ Take the white ribbon and wrap it several times round the symbol, knotting it lightly once and saying:
  Though I cannot go with you in body, yet do I enfold you with my lasting care.

✧ Place the symbol in a small box with some of the rose petals or pot pourri and keep it with your personal treasures.

✧ If the person has died, you can continue to celebrate their birthday or some special shared anniversary by taking the symbol out of the box and lighting a candle on the appropriate day. Replace the petals at this time.

Chapter 5
Social Spells

In the modern, frantic world women especially can feel that life is divided between work and chores. But our friendships not only help us to relax and be ourselves for a while, but also offer us support through all kinds of crises. Family gatherings and outings too (see also pages 83–7) can remind us who and what we are working for. Finally, unless we live miles from anywhere, most of us are dependent on the goodwill of our neighbours, even if they are not the caring, sharing individuals of the daily soap operas. Indeed, noisy or anti-social neighbours can make home life very difficult. All these areas can be improved by spell-casting and can generate good will and pleasure.

Social spell correspondences

Candles: Orange for confidence; yellow for joy; green for family togetherness; pink for friends and reconciliation; red for injecting new life into your social world.

Incenses and oils: Apple blossom, avocado, bay, carnation, geranium, hyacinth, lavender, lily, marigold, mimosa and rose for family occasions, friendship and peace; ferns and ginger for excitement; orange for self-confidence.

Crystals: Blue lace agate, aventurine, jade, moonstone and rose quartz for kind words and honest actions; amber and carnelian for self-confidence; chrysoprase and coral for balanced emotions; obsidian for letting go of old and current resentments; clear quartz crystals, jaspers and malachite for positive but lively energies.

Best time: Social spells are best cast on a Monday or Tuesday if they are for positive improvements in social life.

A spell for a great party

Whatever the occasion, the vital ingredients are good food and drink, and a lively atmosphere.

This spell will create a mixture of lively and harmonising vibes so that there is plenty of fun and laughter, but no flare-ups as perhaps alcohol starts to talk, rivalries emerge or, especially with teenage parties, damage occurs through carelessness. A good party is like a simmering casserole, full of good ingredients that never bubble over.

You will need: Two gentle jade or rose quartz crystals, paired with the more lively jaspers or carnelians, two lively ginger or ginger and orange incense sticks, paired with the softer lavender or lilac, two gentle green and two vibrant yellow or red candles. You can use any of the incenses and crystals listed if you prefer.

Best time: An hour or so before the first guests arrive.

The spell

◈ Work in the main area where guests will be or pass through if it is a garden party.

◈ In the centre of the wall nearest the North, set one of your gentle candles, incense sticks and crystals. Place the crystal in front of the candle in each of the four main directions. You can use small tables or set the items on the floor if there are no children or pets around.

◈ In the East place a vibrant candle, incense stick and crystal, in the South another vibrant trio and finally in the West the three remaining gentle ones.

◈ Begin in the North, lighting first the candle, then the incense stick from the candle. Say:
Bring affection and stability, calm and security to this party and to all who gather here.

◈ Light next the East candle and from it the incense stick, saying:
Bring liveliness and joy, originality and positive communication to this party and all who gather here.

◈ Light next the candle of the South and from it the incense stick, and say:
Bring joy and light, life and abundance to this party and all who gather here.

◈ Light the West candle and from it the gentle incense, and say:
Bring affection and gentleness, kindness and consideration to this party and all who gather here.

✧ Leave the candles and incense to burn down and then, when they are empowered with candlelight and incense smoke, set the four crystals either beneath furniture or under the carpet in the centre of each wall. If it is a teenage party you might like to weight the odds by adding an extra gentle crystal or two in the North and West to preserve stability and calm.

✧ Keep a supply of gentle and enlivening incense sticks so that you can light them in a safe place to change the balance if a party is either slow going or takes off too soon.

A spell for increasing social confidence

The secret of a good social life is to believe in yourself and to exude self-confidence. You will notice that it is often the person whose aura or psychic energy field exudes 'I am likeable' vibes who is surrounded by people. It has taken me many years to overcome my natural shyness, along with rather a lot of put-downs from less than loving partners. This spell requires you to go against the things you were told as a child about modesty and not pushing yourself forward. Unfortunately these rules have led many nice people to undervalue themselves.

You will need: Some modelling clay, a tub of clear glass nuggets or tiny quartz crystals, a bowl filled with red petals or a red, strongly fragranced pot pourri, some ginger essential oil or some ginger or another spicy cooking essence.

Best time: Noon on as sunny a day as possible near to the day of the full Moon.

The spell

- ✧ Work outdoors, in a pool of light if it is sunny, on a small table.
- ✧ Using the modelling clay, create a featureless figure to represent your essential self and all its potential.
- ✧ Begin to press the glass nuggets or crystals into the clay figure, one by one, naming a strength or positive quality you possess for each. Include your physical, emotional and mental good points.
- ✧ If you find this difficult, pretend you are talking about a friend and really try to show him or her in a good light. Sell yourself to the cosmos and most of all to yourself, pressing hard to embed each quality into the clay representation.
- ✧ When you have finished and there is no more space on the figure or no more crystals, say:
  I am special, I am worthy of love and friendship, I have much to offer others and so they value me.
- ✧ Scatter red petals or pot pourri into the air over the figure, saying:
  So do I send myself into the world that those who will make me happy, will seek me out.
- ✧ Leave the crystal figure where it will not be poked by children, sniffed by dogs or thrown away, somewhere high up where the air and light can flow around it.

A spell for meeting new friends

When we change jobs, move to another area or enter a permanent relationship, it can mean losing touch with friends and colleagues with whom we share a social life. Even the most socially confident person has to start again, perhaps breaking into an established social network of people who have known one another for years. If you move to a big city, it can be even harder to meet friendly faces. A relationship break-up can also see old friends disappearing because of divided loyalties. I know when I became a single parent my social life narrowed overnight from the mundane to the non-existent. A woman who gives up work to have a baby can also feel isolated, especially in a small community where there may not be many other young mothers with similar interests.

A spell will help to send out vibes to like-minded people, in much the same way that a spell can attract love.

You will need: A pool of water, three small clear quartz crystals or clear glass nuggets and a dish to hold the crystals. If you cannot find a pool of water, you can work with a large bowl or tub of water in the garden.

Best time: The crescent Moon on the evening it first appears in the sky or the first clear night afterwards. Work just after nightfall.

The spell

- ❖ Stand or sit next to the pool of water so that you are facing the Moon.
- ❖ Hold the first crystal in your power hand, the one you write with. Turn the crystal over three times, and say:
  New Moon, true Moon, bring to me friendship soon and company.
- ❖ Gently cast the crystal towards the centre of the water so that it makes ripples before it sinks. Say:
  Ripple outwards and extend the circle of friendship around me, to surround me that I may no longer be alone.
- ❖ When the ripples have subsided, wait a few moments and visualise people coming towards you, hands outstretched in greeting.
- ❖ Take the second crystal and turn it three times over in your power hand, repeating the Moon rhyme.
- ❖ Cast it slightly further away than the first crystal and repeat the water chant as the ripples appear.
- ❖ When the ripples have gone, wait again and visualise the people moving even closer. You may identify one or two of the faces as people you have already met briefly, perhaps at work or at a local centre. Alternatively they may be people who will come into your life soon.
- ❖ Take the final crystal and turn it over three times, repeating the Moon rhyme before casting it into the water and repeating the water chant.

✧ Add:
Bring friendship before the Moon is done. I ask and so it shall become.

A spell for reviving or mending an old friendship

When we are young, it seems as if we will remain friends with the people we knew at school, college or our first job forever. But as the years go by and we move and change lifestyles, we can lose touch with old friends.

Sometimes this is a good thing, as we may no longer have anything in common. Generally, however, there are a few people from our early life, whose company and concern we value and who have shared our key moments. With pressure of work and sheer distance we can lose contact with these special people, except for a card at Christmas.

We may lose touch with other friends as the result of misunderstandings or pressure from other people. Rifts may have developed and never been mended. Then we suddenly think of them and miss them. The following spell is a way of psychically building or rebuilding emotional bridges. I have adapted the chant from a beautiful CD called 'Chanting' that can be bought from the Museum of Witchcraft in Cornwall (The Harbour, Boscastle, Cornwall, PL35 0HD, Graham King, 01840 250111). If you ever get a chance to visit the museum it is absolutely fascinating and run by friendly and totally non-spooky people.

This is also a good general reconciliation spell.

You will need: A pen and paper, a small set of children's Lego bricks and a photograph of yourself and the lost friend. If you do not have a suitable photograph, then write your name and your friend's name in a continuous circle on a piece of paper.

Best time: Early morning.

The spell

✧ First write your name on one piece of paper and your friend's on another. Place the pieces of paper about 15 cm/ 6 in apart with the photograph or circle of names in between the two. Then place one brick on top of your name and a second brick on top of the name of your friend. Set a third brick over the photograph or circle of names.

✧ Chant softly and mesmerically:
Building bridges between our divisions, I reach out to you and you reach out to me. Putting aside all our divisions, let us rediscover our lost company, let us rediscover our lost company.

✧ As you chant, continue to add to the three towers in turn until they are each three or four blocks high. Then begin to join the towers, working first from your side to the middle, then from the other side to the middle.

✧ When the bridge is completed, rest your hand on the centre pillar and speak softly the words you would like to say to your friend.

✧ Carefully take the bridge apart and put the bricks, the photograph and names together in a box near the telephone, your workspace at home or your computer if you are going to e-mail to re-establish connection.

✧ Repeat the chant before initiating contact.

A spell for improving your social life

What starts as a good arrangement can become a habit: Wednesday at the sports centre, Friday nights at the local wine bar meeting friends, Sunday lunch with your parents or his. Suddenly you may feel like a change. This fire spell is a good way of generating a little excitement and widening your horizons psychically so that new social opportunities come your way and you get the chance to meet different people and to join in new activities.

You will need: A very large red pillar candle and large metallic plate or tray to support it, an egg timer, stop watch or a cookery timer, three sticks of ginger incense or another spicy fragrance, pen and paper and a small quantity of salt in a dish.

Best time: Noon, if possible on the day the full Moon is due as this is a good time for kicking over the traces and bringing positive change into your life.

The spell

◇ Light your red pillar candle, if possible in a pool of natural light.

◇ Set the timer for three minutes, light the first incense stick and, without pausing to think, write a list of places you would like to go on your days off and weekends. Some will be impractical, but others quite attainable given a little rearrangement.

◇ When the three minutes are finished, reset the timer, light the second stick of incense and this time, again without stopping to think, write down those activities you would like to take up either alone or with friends or family.

◇ After this three minutes, again reset the timer, light the third incense stick and this time write the names of people you would like to spend more time with and those you would sooner see less often.

◇ When this final three minutes is finished take a pinch of salt and drop it in the candle flame so that it sparkles and say: *New places, new people, new activities, flame and flare into my life. I call you in the light, ignite.*

◇ Blow out the candle and sit in the sunlight, reading your lists and marking any options that are possible right away and those you will need to introduce gradually.

A spell for happy family outings

My own children talk with fondness of the happy outings we enjoyed when they were young. Some of these I recall in less rose-tinted hues, the car sickness, the rain, the children locked in unarmed combat and me reaching for the headache tablets by coffee time. But obviously there is some reality in their memories. Among the best times was when we went, on the spur of the moment, to the seaside on a rainy November Saturday afternoon for an impromptu camping trip in the motor caravan, buying food and toothbrushes en route.

This spell will minimise hassles and bring to the fore the positive aspects of the prospective trip.

You will need: A photograph of the family in the familiar location you are visiting again or a brochure or an advertisement for the place you intend to discover for the first time, a symbol for the method of transport, for example a toy car, enough clear quartz crystals or clear glass nuggets to make a circle of touching crystals round the picture and symbol, a fibre optic or table lamp that casts a powerful glow, some food treats that will be shared by all the family, either on the journey or soon after arrival.

Best time: The evening before the trip.

The spell

✧ Set the brochure or photograph and on top of it the symbol of transport on a small table.

✧ Moving in a clockwise direction and making sure that each crystal touches those next to it, make a circle around the picture and symbol, saying softly over and over:
Within this circle of love, let nothing bad or sad, angry or spiteful, sharp or dangerous enter. Let the light shine upon our family as we set out upon our adventure.

✧ Switch on the light and let the glow illuminate the crystals.

✧ Again moving in a clockwise direction, now add an outer circle round the crystals, made of sweets, wrapped biscuits, miniature chocolate bars, small cartons of juice, snack cheeses, pieces of fruit or other easily transportable popular snacks. You can use a mixture of items. Make sure that each item touches those next to it in the circle, and say:
May the light fill this circle of nourishment that only kind words, caring actions, laughter and joyous experiences fill the day to come as we set out upon our adventure.

✧ Name each member of the family, including yourself, who is going on the trip and then say for each name:
Bless and protect (name of person) and fill him/her with joy and laughter.

✧ Switch off the lamp and collect the food items, arranging them in sealed containers or bags to be eaten on the journey and during the day.

✧ Place the empowered brochure or photograph and the symbol of transport either with the travel tickets or in the glove compartment of the car.

✧ Just before the trip hold the brochure or photo in one hand and the travel symbol in the other and say in your mind:
Let the light shine upon our family as we set out on our adventure. Love, light, laughter and loveliness, so I bless us all.

A spell for a major family celebration

Whether a christening, a major birthday, a wedding or an anniversary, a formal family celebration is a time of joy and one for renewing family bonds through the focus of a particular landmark event. It can, as with all family get-togethers, also be a time for tensions and rivalry between different branches of the clan.

In Native North American celebrations, the 'give away' was an important part of some collective ceremonies when those invited would be given presents by the host tribe. In Northern European, Scandinavian and Mediterranean lands, the fairies or women of fate came to the christening to offer their good wishes and endow talents upon the new infant.

The idea of presenting each family member with a small gift that is the same for everyone helps to raise the collective energies of affection. Do not forget an item for yourself. You can make the gift relevant to the occasion, tiny agate eggs for a christening, small candles for a wedding or at Christmas, perhaps a pot of herbs, a few flowers or a crystal. Children will readily appreciate the significance of a grown up gift that for once is not to be played with, but taken home to treasure.

You will need: A central pink candle, a long taper and small white, pink or green nightlights, one for each person present. They usually come in their own foil holders, but as people will be holding them, you need heatproof containers (try heatproof dishes, egg cups or special nightlight holders that are inexpensive and make lovely ornaments at parties). Also a small personal gift for each person.

Best time: Any lull in the festivities. After dusk is best.

The spell

❖ Have a tray of nightlights and holders ready and ask the family to stand in a circle. If you have a large enough circular table the guests can sit round in a circle with the lights on the table in front of them. An adult can hold the light with or for a young child and share the blessing. Dim any other lights.

❖ With a long taper light the central candle and say:
 I light this candle to celebrate (name the event and person/ people who are central to it).

❖ Light the first nightlight with the taper saying:
 This is the light of the family. May it burn always in our hearts.

❖ Pass the taper to the next person, who, if necessary, can re-light it from their candle. They light the next nightlight, repeat the words and pass on the taper. Continue until all the candles are lit.

✧ Each person in turn, after lighting their flame, can make a wish for the person or people whose special occasion it is. The person whose celebration it is can add their own wishes for and thanks to the family.

✧ As everyone goes home, give them their special gift to carry the love of the occasion with them.

A spell for quietening noisy neighbours

I once had a next door neighbour who had a drum kit and amplifier in his small front room and, complete with strobe lighting, would put on his disco for one each night until the small hours. I have heard many similar stories. Most noisy neighbours are not malicious or aggressive, just noisy and, for a time, when asked, will make an effort to keep the blasting stereo or masonry drills to sociable hours.

The best spells for dealing with noisy neighbours are likewise not aggressive or harmful, but merely turn the neighbour's volume down a notch or three. If your own family is a noise hazard, you may like to turn down their volume by adapting the spell (before the neighbours complain).

You will need: A rattle, Tibetan bells or any other kind of bells hanging on a rope. You can buy a rattle from an ethnic store, use a child's one or make one from a plastic bottle filled with dried peas or rice. Alternatively use a small set of wind chimes.

Timing: Whenever the noise begins.

The spell

◆ As soon as loud noise or banging comes from next door or your teenagers, shake your rattle loudly or jangle your bells and say loudly:

Loud and jangling, harsh and tangling, cease your wrangling.

◆ Then start to play the rattle more slowly and gently, saying:

Softer sounding, less resounding, slowly, softly, flow to silence.

◆ Slow the rattle and bells till there is silence (at least on your side of the wall).

◆ If the noise continues, repeat the spell three times in all, each time beginning less loudly.

◆ Repeat the spell when necessary.

◆ For a really difficult case, follow my clairvoyant healer friend Lillian's advice and use a tiny doll, wrap it in cotton wool, send it in your mind to float on the sea of tranquillity and leave it in a drawer with soft clothing for eight hours. Again, repeat when necessary.

Chapter 6
Love Spells

Throughout the centuries and in all cultures from Ancient Egypt to the Orient, spells have been cast for love. In the modern world, people of all ages still want to meet the right person and for the relationship to last through the years. Love second, third or even fourth time around and romance in the later years are no different from the very first time we dream of happy ever afters.

Love spell correspondences

Candles: Silver and green for attracting love, romance and fidelity; pink for gentle love and the rebuilding of trust; red for passion; white for formal love rituals and major change points; silver for all Moon love spells.

Incenses and oils: Bay, basil and ivy for fidelity; cinnamon, ginger and rosemary for passion; lavender and rose for preserving love and gentleness; jasmine, mimosa and ylang ylang for sensuality.

Crystals: Jade and moonstones for first love and romance; rose quartz for gentleness and affection; garnets, emeralds and rubies for committed love.

Best time: Fridays are good for love spells.

A spell for attracting new love

We all have, I believe, a number of people who could make us happy as love partners. Sometimes we just need to send out loving vibes into the cosmos to attract one of those people to move into our sphere. A few weeks later we may meet someone in an unexpected place, or a friend of a friend with whom we instantly connect emotionally. In the following spell, if a lot of pins land in one place on the map, a visit there might hurry things along.

You will need: A map of your city, country or the world if you would like a cosmopolitan lover, a box of pins, a magnet, a pin cushion or square of thick felt, and a silver candle.

Best time: The evening you first see the crescent Moon in the sky.

The spell

✧ Spread your map on a table or on the floor.
✧ Take the box of pins and scatter them over the map, saying:
  Near and far o'er land and sea, a lover true, I call to me.
✧ Hold the magnet in your power hand, the one you write with, and circle it clockwise over the map.
✧ As you do so, chant:
  So do I draw love to me, as pin to magnet may he/she be. So I call my lover true, come before the Moon is new.
✧ Stick your pins in the pincushion, making wishes for your future happiness with each pin as you push it into the cushion.

✦ Place the cushion and the magnet on top of the map on an indoor window ledge or on a table near the window and leave it there until the night of the full Moon.

✦ On the night of the full Moon, the most powerful night in the Moon cycle, light a silver candle and let its light shine on the pin cushion while repeating both of the earlier chants.

✦ Leave the cushion in place until the next new Moon, which is two or three days before the crescent appears.

✦ If necessary, repeat the spell the following month.

A spell for turning friendship into love

Many people, especially when making a relationship second or third time around, find love with someone who is an acquaintance, friend or a colleague. The change from friendship to love is just a matter of beginning to look through the eyes of love. Relationships that grow out of friendship or mutual interests are especially likely to succeed. So if you have your eye on an acquaintance, invite him or her to meet you in the evening. Then, before you go, carry out the spell.

You will need: Rose or ylang ylang essential oil or shower gel or dried rose petals, five small pink and green candles or nightlights, two rose or jasmine incense sticks.

Best time: The night before the day of the full Moon if possible. The spell should be carried out before you meet your desired lover for an evening.

The spell

✧ Have a bath to which you have added a few drops of rose or ylang ylang essential oil or dried rose petals (in a net or an old pair of tights so that they do not clog up the bath).

✧ Illuminate the bathroom with pink and green candles and light rose and jasmine incense.

✧ Focus on the pools of light in the bath and splash the light on to your skin, saying:
Look through the eyes of love, at this light within me that burns for you. Look at me through the eyes of love that you may yearn for me, more than friend, as lover, heart to heart, mind to mind and soul to soul, now and through the years.

✧ You can adapt the ritual if you only have a shower by rubbing circles of gel instead of the light water into your skin.

✧ Swirl each pool of light in turn, with your fingers, naming the gifts you bring, for example:
I bring you a gentle heart that will share your joys and sorrows and never condemn you if you fail.

✧ When you have finished naming the gifts, get out and, before you dry yourself, look into the bathroom mirror, with the candlelight behind you.

✧ Call your love through the glass:
Friend more than friend, lover I would be, come now in love, within the glass, lover I would see.

✧ Brush your hair a hundred times as you recite the words more and more softly until they fade into silence.

❖ Keep looking at the mirror through half-closed eyes. Visualise your lover behind you framed in light and on the hundredth brush stroke, call your lover's name.

❖ Close your eyes, open them, blink and you will see him/her either in the glass or in your mind.

❖ Extinguish the candles one by one, sending each shaft of light as a loving feeling. Leave only one illuminated as you dry yourself.

❖ Carry the incense and the remaining candle into your bedroom while you get ready and as you leave, whisper your lover's name once more, saying

Thus in love I speak your name. Come to me now in candle flame.

❖ Blow out the candle and go to meet him or her.

A spell for moving in together or planning marriage

The time comes in a relationship when one or both partners are ready to move into a home together or to talk about marriage. One party may hesitate, not through lack of love, but perhaps because of a previous failed relationship. In the case of younger people, the benefits of room service in the family home – and the additional financial freedom – may prove an incentive to leave a relationship as it is. If this is the case, a spell can sometimes generate the energies for the hesitant partner to move to the next stage. Even if both of you are equally committed, the spell can make the transition easier and launch the new stage with positive energies.

You will need: A green candle, a gold or silver dress ring (choose one with a tiny genuine or imitation diamond, emerald or ruby if you would like to become engaged), salt, some water in which you have soaked a tiny rose quartz or jade crystal, a square of green cloth and green twine.

Best time: Any evening during the waxing Moon period.

The spell

◇ Light a green candle and hold the dress ring above the flame.

◇ Circle the flame three times clockwise with the ring, saying:
Round and round the ring of truth, love in age and love in youth, love in sickness and in health, love in dearth and love in wealth.

◇ Place the ring in front of the candle.

◇ Next surround the ring with a circle of salt sprinkled clockwise. As you make the circle, say:
Come, my love, and stay with me. Stay if it is right to be.

◇ Finally sprinkle a few drops of the empowered water round the ring and say:
Come, my love, and with me stay, stay for ever and a day.

◇ Gaze into the candle flame and speak private words of love to the person you wish to marry or move in with.

✧ Blow out the candle, visualising the light travelling to where your loved one is at the time of the spell, encircling him or her in longing to be with you.

✧ Whisper into the darkness:
  Come, my love, and with me stay, stay for ever and a day.

✧ Wrap the crystal, the salt you used and the ring in the green cloth, bind it with green twine, using three knots to secure the parcel and bury it either in a deep flower pot beneath a fast growing herb or in the garden, preferably beneath a rose bush.

A spell for bringing passion into a relationship

This is a powerful spell whether you cast it before you consummate a relationship for the first time or if you are trying to conceive a baby and have become locked in a passion-destroying routine of ovulation charts and hospital visits. However, it is also good for busy working couples who have lost touch with each other

You might need temporarily to rearrange the bedroom a little.

You will need: A small bowl of dried rose petals or rose-based pot pourri, a ginger or cinnamon incense stick, a red candle, a crystal, glass or metal goblet, some mineral water and four small tables.

Best time: After dusk.

The spell

◇ Just after dusk, place the small bowl of rose petals or pot pourri on a small table at the head of the bed.

◇ Light a stick of cinnamon or ginger incense and set it on a small table to the left of the bed about half-way down.

◇ At the bottom of the bed set a red candle on another small table.

◇ Finally to the right of the bed about half-way down on the fourth table, place a glass or a goblet of pure mineral water.

◇ Take the pot pourri and, beginning at the bed head, move clockwise in a complete circle round the bed, scattering a little of the pot pourri or petals on the floor. As you do so, say:
  I call my love with the power of Earth.

◇ Take the incense stick and make another complete clockwise circle of the bed, making a smoke trail and saying:
  I call my love with the power of Air.

◇ Pick up the candle and make a third clockwise circle round the outside of the bed, saying:
  I call my love with the power of Fire.

◇ Finally sprinkle a few drops of the water in a clockwise circle, saying:
  I call my love with the power of Water.

◇ Sit in the centre of the bed facing the door.

◇ Make circles over the bed with your hands, palms down, the left circling clockwise and the right anticlockwise at the same time. (Practise this before the spell to get the rhythm.) This is an old method of enchantment.

✧ Recite continuously as you enchant the bed:
Earth, Air, Water, Fire, make him/her only me desire. Earth Water, Fire and Air, make him/her for me only care. Air, Water, Fire and Earth, thus I ask, give passion birth.

✧ Chant faster and faster until your hands seem to spin, and end with the cry:
Earth, Air, Water, Fire.

✧ If you want to have a baby you can end the chant with:
Earth, Air, Fire and Water, bring to me a son or daughter.

✧ Blow out the candle and call out:
Passion be, power I free.

✧ Leave the incense to burn down and close the door.

A fidelity spell

This spell can be helpful if you have hit a rocky patch in a long-term relationship or if you or your partner go away a great deal. It is a way of preserving the spiritual and emotional bond when you are not able to spend time together.

Ivy is an ancient fidelity symbol, regarded in folklore as the wife and Queen of the ancient Holly King and a token of lasting love.

With fidelity spells you have to be very careful not to bind someone against their will. They are useful, however, in the modern world where working couples especially may travel for days or even weeks with only hurried mobile phone calls to keep in touch.

If you do not have time for a spell, sprinkle a circle of dried cooking basil around your partner's case or stick a few grains in the bottom of one of the pockets of the travel bag.

You will need: A strand of ivy or another plant such as honeysuckle that entwines around trees or buildings. Also two tiny cloth or wooden dolls, the kind you can buy in ethnic gift shops (or model them from clay), jasmine or rose incense, a small undyed straw basket or a tiny doll's cradle, and dried basil. Also a small cloth bag and dried rose petals or rose pot pourri.

Best time: Dusk.

The spell

✧ At twilight, take a strand of ivy and two tiny cloth or wooden dolls.

✧ Bind the dolls loosely face to face with the trailing plant, being careful not to break the twine. If it does break, pick some more.

✧ Light a jasmine or rose incense stick and weave fronds of smoke around the ivy, creating nine smoke knots. As you do so, say:

Ivy, ivy, plant of love, keep my lover true, willingly myself I bind, and thus our vows renew.

✧ Put the two dolls in the straw basket into which you have sprinkled a little basil.

✧ Over the basket repeat your marriage vows or make pledges of your fidelity.

✧ Leave the basket until day break in a sheltered outdoor place or on a balcony where it cannot get wet.

✧ In the morning unbind the dolls and place them face to face in a small cloth bag, filled with dried rose petals or rose pot pourri. Keep the bag in a drawer near your bed.

✧ Replace the pot pourri when it loses its fragrance, and weave smoke knots over the purse, renewing the pledges whenever one of you goes away.

A two-day sea spell for winning a lover back

If a lover behaves badly whether through being unfaithful, feckless or untrustworthy in other ways you need to decide before carrying out the spell if you would be happier without him or her.

However, it may be that it was circumstance or the malice of others that contributed to or even caused the problem. So the spell can also help against interfering relations who may have their own reasons for breaking up the relationship or those who get pleasure from deliberately seducing people in relationships.

This spell is based on an old ritual in which sailors' wives took water from the sea when their husbands left and then poured it back when the ship was expected, saying:

Lady Ocean, Mother Sea, I return what is yours, return mine to me.

You will need: Water from the sea or an unpolluted water source (river or canal), a flower and a bottle with a screw cap.

Best time: As early in the morning as possible. If you are using the sea, you want to be there for the incoming tide on the first day, and the outgoing tide on the second day.

The spell

✧ Go to your water source and scoop up water into your bottle. As you do so, say:

Lady Ocean, Mother Sea (or Lady Water, River free), I take this with humility, as token of he/she for whom I lack, I ask that he/she may soon come back.

✧ On the seventh wave (or after counting seven on the river bank), cast a flower into the water and speak the words you would like to say to your departed love. These words will be carried on the water.

✧ Put on the lid of the bottle. Set aside your problems and unhappiness and focus on a series of small steps to make the day happy.

✧ Next day, return to your water source.

✧ Pour back the water and say:

Lady Ocean, Mother Sea (or Lady Water, River free) I return what is yours, send mine back to me.

✧ Call the name of your lost love as loudly as you can so it is carried by the water to where your lost love is.

✧ Take something small home with you, a stone, a shell or a

tiny piece of driftwood and place it with any of your lover's belongings or a memento he/she gave you.

✧ If practical and you feel able, try to make some reconciliatory gesture. If it fails, then you know you have done all you can.

A spell for renewing trust or ending a period of coldness or anger

After a bad quarrel with a partner or lover or a long period of silence it can be hard to let the bitterness or guilt go and to get positive feelings flowing again. Ice spells are not surprisingly very popular in Scandinavia, Russia and Canada, and are a powerful way of melting ice from around the heart. This also works well after family quarrels (see pages 59–61).

You will need: A small heatproof bowl, ice from the fridge or freezer or snow if it is lying on the ground, a wooden spoon, very small pink candles, rose quartz crystals or pink glass nuggets, a small net or scoop and another small bowl.

Best time: During the period of the waning Moon or the hour after sunset.

The spell

✧ Fill a small heatproof bowl with ice.

✧ Gently stir the ice with a wooden spoon, naming the resentment, fury or unspoken words that are bubbling inside and the positive feelings that have become frozen inside you. Literally 'put them on ice'.

✧ Make a circle of alternate tiny pink candles and rose quartz crystals or pink glass nuggets around the bowl. Light the candles and say:

Ice go, water flow, take from me this misery.

✧ Stir the ice again and feel it softening.

✧ Keep stirring as the ice melts, visualising a pink glow rising from the candles and crystals and mingling with the white energy field of the ice surrounding the bowl.

✧ Name all the positive aspects of the person, situation or relationship, however difficult this may be. It can be helpful to imagine you are in the other person's shoes.

✧ When you have finished, sit in the candlelight, recalling happier times, memories of shared jokes, holidays, times when you did act in unison.

✧ When the ice has melted, stir the water, saying:

Water flow, sorrows go, leaving only harmony.

✧ Drop your crystals or nuggets one by one into the water, making a wish for happier times with each one. After each wish try to think of a step you can take to improve things.

✧ Leave the crystals in the water as the candles burn down and take practical steps to improve communication: a phone call, inviting the estranged person to share a favourite meal, booking a weekend away for the two of you if you are still involved but not talking.

✧ When the candles have burned down, scoop out the crystals in a tiny net or with your hands and leave them in a small bowl to dry naturally.

✧ Tip away the water down a drain, saying:
Go from me, flow from me, leaving only harmony.

✧ After you have met the person, light a pink candle and circle it with the empowered crystals to amplify the good feelings.

A spell for ending love

If a relationship cannot be mended and is perpetually cold or destructive, it may be better to part. But that can be difficult especially if the relationship has existed for years or your partner is controlling and has convinced you the problems are of your making. In such a case it is hard to leave, as self-confidence can plummet with a persistently unfaithful or abusive lover.

However, even a destructive relationship is better finished gently on your part and with dignity.

Cutting or burning a cord is a useful symbolic action in a spell for separating because in the old custom of hand fasting, couples beginning married life would tie their hands together with a cord to symbolise unity.

You will need: A length of thin, red curtain cord (about 25 cm/10 in) and a sharp knife.

Best time: If possible, on the waning Moon or late at night.

The spell

✧ Hold the curtain cord and in your mind endow it with all the negative emotions, the anger, fear, hurt and regrets of the dying relationship.

✧ Say:
The cord is long. The cord between us was strong, but now is decaying, fraying, breaking.

✧ Cut the cord in half with the knife, saying:
No more one, we are two. The cord is broken.

✧ If possible, burn one half of the cord on an outside bonfire or an open fire. If not, bury it in a deep hole with the words:
It is gone, it is done, peace come.

✧ Put the other half of the cord in a drawer.

✧ The next night, take the remaining length of cord and repeat the words, cutting the cord in half and again discarding the part that falls on the floor, saying once more:
No more one, we are two. The cord is broken.

✧ Continue nightly until only a short length of cord remains, then burn this final piece.

✧ If matters are complex, you may need more cords over the weeks that follow, but each time begin with a shorter one.

Chapter 7
Money Spells

It is not materialistic to cast spells for your money needs. After all, you are unlikely to be able to concentrate on healing the planet or helping others if you have money worries. Enough for your needs and a little more is the rule of magic. You may need a holiday to recharge your batteries; that is a realistic need. If, however, you start specifying five star and club class, that may be stretching the generosity of the cosmos. However, I have found that by doing money spells I have managed to escape from a few tight corners.

The principle of money spells is that by the process known as sympathetic or attracting magic, you can symbolically grow money and then, by doing a spell, transfer the money energies you generate to the realm of actuality.

The down, or you may see it as up, side is that what you receive from the cosmic money pot you have to pay back whether in time or effort or in helping some worthwhile project or person when you have the spare cash. This might be anything from setting up a table for wild birds in your garden to planting a tree in an urban woodland scheme or sending a few extra pounds for a school trip so that a child whose parents do not have spare money at the time can go along.

Money spell correspondences

Candles: Yellow for an urgent or sudden need for money and for ventures involving speculation; green for the steady growth of prosperity; blue for the conservation of wealth; gold for major money-generating schemes or large amounts.

Incenses and oils: Allspice, basil, cinnamon and ginger for acquiring money fast; bay and patchouli for steady growth; frankincense, neroli and sage for bringing a new money source into your life and for grandiose schemes.

Crystals: Amber, tiger's eye and peridot for prosperity; metallic crystals such as haematite, lodestone, polished iron pyrites for all forms of money-making; silver, copper and gold, especially as coins, for instant money or a gradual inflow of wealth.

Best time: Wednesday is the best day for money spells.

A basic money spell

This incredibly simple money spell is nevertheless one of the most powerful I know. Therefore it should only be used sparingly and should be saved for real crises. You need to be specific about the amount you actually need – the more precise you are, the better the spell seems to work.

You will need: A money candle (the square kind with a lucky Chinese coin embedded within it) or a beeswax candle and a small coin that you can press into the wax before the spell. You may need to warm the candle slightly to do this.

Best time: Any time when the need is urgent.

The spell

✧ Light the candle and gaze into the flame. Say six times in rapid succession:

Five hundred pounds (or however much you need), it surrounds, it compounds, it astounds me.

✧ On the final chant, blow out the candle and call out the amount of money you need.

✧ If things are really dire you can repeat the chant nine times.

✧ Then do nothing. Deliberately push away calculations or concerns about the money. Let the spell work in its own way and do not repeat it for at least a fortnight.

A spell for the regular flow of money or the gradual increase of prosperity

For most of us, the main issue is to ensure a regular flow of money that increases over the months and years. There can be all kinds of reasons why this flow is interrupted or reduced, working part-time when a baby is born, moving to a more satisfying but less lucrative career, redundancy or job loss.

The spell works on the principle of generating money energies that are slower acting but longer lasting than those created by the previous spell. By carrying it out every month or so you can top up your money sources. Salt is a frequent component of money spells since it is essential for life and in earlier times was a valuable commodity because of the necessity of preserving food through the winter.

You will need: Salt, a metal tray, a green candle in a holder, a small spoon, twelve coins, one for each month, a small glass dish filled with still mineral water and a pot or jar with a lid.

Best time: From the day of the crescent Moon, if possible.

The spell

✧ Make a small pile of salt in the centre of the metal tray and surround it with a circle of coins.

✧ Light your green candle in its holder and set it on the tray so that the light shines on the salt and the coins. Say:
Money grow, light flow, bring to me prosperity.

✧ Repeat the chant five more times and then blow out the candle, picturing the light flowing into the salt and the coins.

✧ Re-light the candle, gather up the coins and set them in the pot without its lid in front of the candle.

✧ Scoop up the salt spoonful by spoonful into the bowl of water and stir it until it dissolves. Tip the salt water down a sink or drain under running water. Say:
Money flow free, flow to me, from the rivers and the sea, bringing me prosperity.

✧ Leave the candle to burn down and then place the pot holding the coins, and with its lid on, in a warm place in the kitchen or a sunny part of the house.

✧ Each day add a single coin, saying:
Money grow, money flow, bring to me prosperity.

✧ If you hit a glitch, burn a green candle over the pot.

A spell to stop money flowing out of your life

Even if you do usually have enough money coming into the household, there can be periods when there is one demand after another for unexpected expenses: new tyres for the car, a broken down washing machine or a vet bill for the family pet. If you have children, there may be non-stop requests for trainers to replace worn out or misplaced ones, for school trips or for driving lessons.

Knot magic is especially powerful for stopping money slipping away and minimising unexpected minor financial disasters by blocking the psychic outflow.

You will need: A deep blue candle (the colour of stability), a long, blue cord or ribbon, a small padlock and chain (an old one will do) and an old box.

Best time: Any time you need it, but the waxing Moon is good.

The spell

✧ Light your blue candle and singe both ends of the cord, saying:
   Cut off the flow, money no more outward go.
✧ Tie a knot about a quarter of the way down the cord, saying:
   Knot one, I make, the flow I break, thus I bind, money find, within this knot.
✧ Tie a second knot half-way down the cord, saying:
   Knot two, I make, the flow I break, accumulate, within this knot.

❖ Tie a third knot three quarters of the way down the cord, saying:
  Knot three, I make, the flow I break, thus I bind, money wind, within this knot.

❖ Tie the two ends of the cord together to make a circle, saying:
  Knot four, the last, bad luck is past, money bound tight, all is right.

❖ Place the knotted cord inside the box and secure with the padlock. Keep it in a place where you normally work out your finances or sign cheques to pay bills.

A spell for winning competitions and attracting financial luck

Some people have amazing luck and often win competitions, not always star prizes, but weekends away, cases of wine or free admission to cinemas. When I was young, one of the first television quiz masters used to end his show by saying: 'Think lucky and you'll be lucky'. In a sense he was right, because the luckier you feel, the more good luck follows, like a giant snowball.

You will need: A money crystal, such as a tiger's eye or the kind of iron pyrites that looks like a piece of gold, or, alternatively, a small, gold-coloured lucky charm or a gold earring. Silver doesn't work so well for this spell. Also two gold candles and a gold-coloured dish filled with all the small gold-coloured items you can find. You can use gold-coloured Christmas baubles, brass, gold foil, gold or gold-plated jewellery, gold coins and small pieces of golden fruit. If you don't have a golden dish, cover one with gold foil or substitute a clear glass one.

Best time: The day of the full Moon, if possible at noon.

The spell

✧ Find a pool of sunlight or if it is dark use mirrors or a fibre optic lamp to create a circular area of light.

✧ Set your golden dish in the centre of the light and set the two gold candles on either side of it.

✧ Light the candles, saying:
Gold of fortune, good luck shine, Lady Luck, make fortune mine.

✧ Pile your gold objects on to the dish, saying:
Gold of fortune, increased be, Lady Luck, smile down on me.

✧ Hold your crystal in the light and concentrate on a piece of past good fortune, the excitement and the glow of happiness. This is important in setting up the positive connection between you and the crystal.

✧ Place your money crystal right in the centre of the dish on top of all the objects, saying:
Gold of fortune, fill with power, Lady Luck, this crystal shower, bring luck to me when this I see.

✧ Taking a candle in each hand, with care, swirl the light from them around the dish in spirals, chanting:
  Light of gold intensify, power of luck multiply, from the earth to the sky, nothing now can me deny.
✧ Extinguish the candles and leave the gold dish and the objects with the crystal on top right through the day. If the night is clear allow the full Moon to shine on it too.
✧ At noon, eat the fruit. By this time, the crystal will be filled with power. Place it on any competition forms as you fill them in and carry it in a purse whenever you compete or speculate.

A spell for helping savings to accumulate

In the mid west of America, families traditionally had a money pot that was kept near the family hearth and was added to each day. This same idea is used in this spell to increase the money flow. It can also be adapted to increase savings potential.

You will need: A large jar with a lid, a green candle, some dried bay leaves (the kind you cook with) in a sealed pot, and a coin you have found around the house.

Best time: Any but the waxing Moon gives you a good start.

The spell
✧ Unusually, start this spell with a rule that the family are not to borrow from the money jar for small change. The bay leaves will act as a good deterrent.

✧ Begin by psychically warming the jar by lighting your green candle close to it.

✧ Put the coin in the jar and then add a bay leaf, saying:
Accumulate, make more, two make into four, accumulate and wait, four will become eight.

✧ Blow out the candle and repeat:
Save and prosper so do I/we.

✧ Put the lid on the jar and leave it in a warm place in the kitchen or living room next to the sealed pot of bay leaves.

✧ Every time you find a coin around the house, in the bottom of your bag or in the glove compartment of the car, put it in the money jar, adding a bay leaf and repeating the chant.

✧ When the jar is full, remove the bay leaves and if necessary wash the money if it is dusty.

✧ Bank the money in a special savings account and it will accumulate over the months. You will find other saving potentials are attracted by sympathetic magic.

A spell to help yourself or family members with debt problems

Debts can accumulate because we have had to borrow to survive and it is all too easy to end up in a spiral of interest payments that you borrow more to keep up with. Redundancy, illness and the break up of partnerships can all add to debt problems. First you should seek sensible worldly help: a Citizens' Advice Bureau rather than a loan shark or consolidation agency. Magic won't make the debts disappear, but it can help you to galvanise your survival energies and to draw a little help from the cosmos that might just make a difference.

You will need: A piece of coloured paper and some white chalk. If it is not raining on the day of the spell, you will also need a bucket of water and some lemon juice.

Best time: The waning Moon is best, but work any time when the need is urgent. Ideally this spell should be done on a rainy day.

The spell

✧ Write on the paper either your fears of the consequences of not paying, or a representative amount you owe (I have to work with very large pieces of paper).

✧ When you have written on your piece of paper, put it out in the rain or in a bucket of water and say:
  Rain, rain, take away, debts that I cannot pay. Rain, rain, wash away, fears that haunt me night and day. Rain, rain, take from me, helplessness and make me free.

✧ When the paper has disintegrated, scoop it up and throw it away. Scrub the area clean or wash out the bucket, adding a little lemon juice.

A spell for making wise purchases and for curbing extravagance

More access to credit and ever-present advertising increase the temptation to buy items that we do not really need. Especially if we have children, we are subject to demands caused by peer pressure to conform to the latest fashion.

If, like me, you are a natural shopaholic because you enjoy it and not through any deep-seated trauma, it can help before a spree or before taking out children, to do this mild binding spell on yourself and anyone whose purchases you will be financing.

You will need: Your credit cards, cheque book or purse containing the spending money, a deep purple ribbon and some purple or blue flowers (silk or dried, or a purple pot pourri are fine if you do not have fresh).

Best time: Twilight any time, but the waning Moon is especially good for binding spells of any kind.

The spell

✧ On the evening before you are going to the shops for a major purchase or a spending spree, make a pile of any credit cards, store cards, cheque books and/or your purse or wallet containing money.

✧ In the ebbing light, circle the pile with the flowers, repeating quietly and calmly until you are totally relaxed:
Wisely spend will quickest mend, shopping is a pleasure.
Wisely spend and soon to end, spending slow a treasure.

✧ Taking the ribbon equally slowly and calmly, bind the pile of cards quite loosely, reciting:
Wisely spend and well, power of binding spell. Wisely spend will soonest mend, of this I now do tell.

✧ Leave the cards and circle of flowers in the darkness overnight.

✧ In the morning gently unbind the ribbon and say:
Thus unbound, but powerful still, free in heart and mind and will. As the cords I now unwind, recklessness I leave behind.

✧ Tie the ribbon inside your bag as a calming influence and touch it if you are about to make a wild and totally unsuitable purchase.

A spell for bringing you what you most need

Under the cosmic exchange rule, when we need a replacement for something, there is generally someone getting rid of a similar thing at the same time. It is just a question of drawing to ourselves, by a process of mind power known as psychokinesis, someone else's surplus. For example, your fax machine may break down at the same time that someone else is moving abroad and is willing to offer it to you for a quick sale. You may lose your mobile phone at the same time that one of your acquaintances or a relation of a work colleague has been given a new one for their birthday.

Of course, in return you have to be prepared to hand on your surplus items to keep the cosmic barter system going. You can also use this method to find goods you need cheaply in a store, perhaps in a closing down sale or as a one-day special offer or shop-soiled model at the back of the store.

You will need: A small square of paper, a pen, a gold or yellow candle, some scissors, a deep, ceramic, fireproof bowl or an old saucepan and a large metal tray.

Best time: Any time after dark, but waxing energies may make the transference easier.

The spell

◇ Draw a picture of the item you need. Create as detailed an image as possible, visualising as you draw, an item that is not state of the art or top of the range, but of the kind that will serve your needs. Endow the picture with your anticipated pleasure and bring the image in your mind closer and closer until you can imagine yourself touching it.

◇ Light your candle behind the drawing and, gazing into the flame, state your need, mentioning the purpose as well as any specifications and exactly when you need it. For example, you might say:
   A word processor to replace mine so I can complete my coursework by the end of the month. I could pay at the most £ ... I would like if possible ...

- ✧ Again recreate the image in your mind, bringing it so close that you could touch it.
- ✧ Write on the back of the drawing your need and the details. Say the words aloud as you write them and place the writing side face up in front of the candle.
- ✧ Say:

  Come to me, as I count three. Three, two, one, the spell's begun.
- ✧ Cut the image into the tiniest pieces that you can and place them in the bowl or saucepan on the metal tray well away from anything that they might set light to.
- ✧ Set fire to the paper, close your eyes, open them, blink and you may see, in the flames or your mind's vision, the object where it is at present or the location of the present owner.
- ✧ If nothing is clear, do not worry, as the circumstances will arise naturally if you follow any impulses to go to a particular place at a certain time.
- ✧ As the paper burns, name your need once more and say:

  Come to me, as I count three. Three, two, one, the prize is won.
- ✧ When the paper is burned, scatter the ashes in the open air, for the final time reciting your need and saying:

  Come to me, as I count three. Three, two, one, the spell is done.

Chapter 8
Career and Work Spells

Our career is an area that can especially benefit from spells of all kinds, both those to attract a good, satisfying job and those to banish problems and negativity from the workplace. Whether you work in a large or small firm, the daily meeting of different personalities, the difference in people's attitudes towards timekeeping, input, meal breaks, domestic emergencies and overtime, can cause tensions as can competition for promotion. If you are self-employed, the stresses and challenges are no less, especially if you work from home. I do, and my family assume that I am always free to give lifts, book doctors' appointments and deal with repair people.

Work spell correspondences

Candles: Blue for all employment issues; yellow for jobs in technology or medicine; orange for the media, also anything to do with art or publishing and working with people; pink for working with children and animals; green for gardening or environmental posts; brown both for business, banks, civil service, government, and also for practical tasks where you will use your hands.

Incenses and oils: Allspice, cinnamon, eucalyptus and ginger for a new job or promotion; geranium, moss and vetivert for a happy workplace; lemongrass, parsley, patchouli, rosemary, sage and thyme for self-employment, new skills and growth of business ventures.

Crystals: Angelite/celestite, blue lace agate, kunzite and sodalite for a calm, happy working atmosphere; citrine, clear quartz crystals, lapis lazuli and falcon/hawk's eye (a blue version of tiger's eye) for a new job or promotion; amethyst, haematite, laboradite and malachite for protection against negativity. Malachite is especially good against adverse effects from computers and technological equipment.

Best time: Thursdays are good for career spells.

A three-day spell for getting a job

Finding a new job is one of the most anxiety-creating and potentially exciting situations we face. It may be a first job after school or college, returning to work after staying at home for a while to care for children or relatives. If you have been unemployed for a while or live in an area of high unemployment, your confidence can plummet. A spell can help to set you back on track and send out vibes to draw work to you.

You will need: A job description of the desired post from a newspaper or job centre leaflet, or paper and pen to write your own job description, three blue candles, a broad-based holder for each candle and a large metal tray.

Best time: If possible, three consecutive nights on the waxing

Moon; best of all are the two nights leading up to the full Moon and the night of the full Moon itself.

The spell

✧ Set the candles and holders on the tray in a horizontal row.

✧ Light the left-hand candle.

✧ Read aloud your job description or write your ideal job details by the light of the candle and read that aloud.

✧ Then say:

I ask for this job, this job is for me, bring us ever closer, ever closer be.

✧ Place the paper on the tray in front of the candle and repeat the chant. Blow out the candle and send light to the place where you would like to work. Leave the job description in front of the candle.

✧ On the second day light the left-hand and the central candles. Repeat the words:

I ask for this job, this job is for me, bring us ever closer, ever closer be.

✧ Read the job description again and place the job description in front of the central candle. Blow out both candles in reverse order of lighting and send the light as before.

✧ On the third day, light all three candles, beginning with the left-hand one, then the central and finally the right-hand one.

✧ Repeat the words and read the job description, then place it in front of the right-hand candle.

✧ This time do not blow out the candles but burn the job description, by passing it through each of the flames in turn, beginning with the one on the left and leaving it on the tray to burn to ashes. Say:

Three times three, the spell is cast, the job I seek is mine at last.

✧ Leave the candles to burn down. Bury the ashes under a living tree or a plant in a tub.

✧ On the fourth morning, if you have not already done so, apply for the job or follow up your application.

A spell for promotion

Even if we are well qualified, an interview or tests for promotion whether within the current firm or another one can be nerve wracking and we can sometimes either forget what we were going to say or appear too eager. A spell on the morning of an interview is a good way of increasing your professional desirability aura or psychic energy vibes and creating a calm, confident centre inside you that radiates outwards.

You will need: A glass bowl, still mineral water, ten tiny clear quartz or sparkling citrine crystals (yellow clear glass nuggets will do) and gold foil.

Best time: As dawn breaks so the morning light can flood the bowl. (You will be too excited or anxious to sleep anyway.)

The spell

✧ The day before the interview, place the ten quartz or citrine crystals in the glass bowl and half-fill the bowl with the mineral water. During the hours of daylight, leave this to absorb the Sun power, outdoors if possible.

✧ At dusk (or as near as you can manage) cover the bowl with gold foil and leave it again, outdoors if you can.

✧ The next morning, take the foil off the bowl. Work outdoors or by a window where the first light will shine in on the water. Place the gold foil at the side of the bowl.

✧ With your fingers, ripple the surface of the water, whispering mesmerically:

Gold of the Sun, flow within me, that my radiance all will see.

✧ Take one of the crystals from the water and hold it in the centre of your hair line, saying:

Inspire me to succeed, by the power of the Sun.

✧ Place it on the foil.

✧ Continue to take crystals from the bowl and when you have used them to empower the different parts of your body, set them on the foil.

✧ Place the second crystal on your brow and say:

Inspire me to confidence, by the power of the Sun.

✧ Place the third and fourth on your eyes, saying:

Inspire me to clear and inspired vision, by the power of the Sun.

✧ Place the fifth and sixth on your ears and say:
Let me listen and understand what I am asked, by the power of the Sun.

✧ Set the seventh on your lips and say in your mind:
Let my words be wise and not stumbling, by the power of the Sun.

✧ Put the eighth on your throat, saying:
Let my ideas be original and relevant to what is needed, by the power of the Sun.

✧ Hold the ninth over your heart and say:
May I be calm and attract positive emotions by my replies, by the power of the Sun.

✧ Hold the tenth over your solar plexus in the centre of your stomach below the rib cage and say:
May I be filled with power and authority in my words and actions, by the power of the Sun.

✧ Leave the crystals to dry and have a bath or shower, adding your Sun water from the bowl to the hot water if you are having a bath, and tipping it over you to mix with the shower water if you are having a shower. Visualise the Sun water entering you and filling you with sparkling gold.

✧ Take the crystals in a purse in your bag with you to the interview. If you panic while waiting to be called, touch each of them and recall in your mind the different powers you drew into yourself.

A spell for a happy and harmonious workplace

Even in the largest workplace there tend to be a key number of people with whom you interact. A happy workplace not only results in increased production, but also avoids absences due to psychosomatic conditions and stress-related minor accidents caused by loss of concentration.

It is possible to neutralise any negativity caused by workplace tensions and even personality clashes by casting a spell to create an aura or psychic energy field of calm and positivity.

Because it is not easy to cleanse an office with crystals or incenses without attracting curious or adverse comment, you can work by the principle of sympathetic or attracting magic, using a plan that shows the key features of the workplace.

You will need: A square of paper, large enough to draw a detailed plan, different coloured marker pens, four geranium or thyme incense sticks for gentle but positive vibes (if you can't get these, substitute the all-purpose lavender). Also a soft blue crystal, such as sodalite or blue lace agate or a pale blue glass nugget to represent each of the key workers, a larger crystal for yourself, a blue candle in a deep holder and a small green plant.

Best time: Any time on the waxing Moon.

The spell

✧ Using the marker pens, draw a plan of the workplace. Draw a separate plan for each floor.

✧ Mark with circles where the key people sit, and with small squares any areas where staff congregate.

✧ Set a crystal or glass nugget on each of the circles.

✧ At the four corners of the plan place your incense sticks in their holders and right in the centre of the plan set the green plant and the candle.

✧ Light the candle, saying:

Light of blue, aura of blue, send your peace on all we do.
Aura of blue, light of calm, keep all within safe from harm.

✧ Breathe in the candlelight slowly and deeply through your nose and visualise yourself filled with soft blue light.

✧ On each out breath, with a sigh through your mouth, gently blow the light all over the plan, picturing it extending over your actual workplace and those who share it with you.

✧ Visualise blue light from the candle also entering the green plant and mingling with its natural energies.

✧ Now light the incense sticks from the candle, starting in the North and moving in a clockwise direction.

✧ Pass the first incense stick that you lit over the plan, creating smoke swirls and saying:

Light of blue, aura of blue, send your peace on all we do.
Aura of blue, light of calm, keep all within safe from harm.

✧ Return the incense to its corner and repeat with the other three incenses.

✧ Leave the candle and incense to burn down.

✧ Repeat the spell with the plan for any other floors.

✧ The next day take the plant to work and set it in your workspace, encircled by the crystals. When things seem fraught or tensions are set to rise, breathe in the blue and green light of the plant and gently blow it on the circle of crystals, naming each key person they represent in your mind and sending them blessings. You will feel the atmosphere lift. You can set your own crystal in the centre next to the plant.

✧ Wash the crystals under a tap at work to restore energies and remember to take great care of your hard-working plant.

A spell for stopping a vicious gossip or troublemaker at work

Even in the friendliest office there may be one person who is always sarcastic or who you know talks about you behind your back. The person may be jealous of you or soured by life and personal disappointment, but such negativity constantly winging your way, even if others are victims too, can leave you exhausted and prone to mistakes and free-floating anxiety.

Under the laws of magic you cannot banish the person or wish them ill as the negativity would rebound. However, you can deflect the venom. A simple device is to leave a small hand mirror or a pair of spectacles in your workspace so that the light will reflect the negativity back to the sender.

This spell is centred on an ancient but effective method of protection, making and empowering an anti-venom bottle. It will deflect negativity almost instantly.

You will need: A small bottle with a cork or lid, sour milk, dried ginger powder or allspice, a few drops of eucalyptus essential oil or a bath foam or shampoo containing eucalyptus.

Best time: As close to the end of the waning Moon cycle as possible.

The spell

✧ Half fill your bottle with sour milk, saying:
   Venom and spite, sourness and viciousness, cease and lose your sting.

✧ Add a few pinches of ginger, allspice or any other spice.

✧ Cork the bottle and shake it vigorously, saying:
   Venom and viciousness, sourness and spite, begone and trouble me no more.

✧ Turn the bottle nine times anticlockwise, saying:
   Turn away your malice and malevolence, your mischievous and unkind mutterings.

✧ Uncork the bottle and, under a running tap, tip away the contents, saying:
   Go in peace, anger cease, trouble not me. Transformed be to healing rain.

✧ Wash out the bottle and the sink with hot water and a little eucalyptus oil until both are cleansed.

✧ Dispose of the bottle where it can be recycled.

✧ Though you did not target your spiteful colleague or boss by name, you will find that you will now be left in peace.

A spell for self-employment and working from home

It can be very exciting to work from home or set up your own business, but also incredibly hard work and very lonely. You need a lot of stamina and optimism, especially in the early days if you cannot afford to employ anyone to help you. Increasing numbers of women especially are combining working from home with bringing up a family, so this is an area where you need a very active positive spell.

You will need: A computer and a simple drawing programme or several sheets of white paper and a black pen.

Best time: When the crescent Moon appears.

The spell

✧ Write your name in the centre of the computer screen or a piece of paper. As you do so, name yourself aloud and what you do or make, for example:
 I am Cassandra and I am an author.

✧ Make the name larger on the screen or write it larger on a second piece of paper, still in the centre. Repeat your name and what you do aloud, twice this time.

✧ Increase the size of the words either on the screen or on a fresh sheet of paper, repeating the empowerment again.

✧ By the seventh or eight attempt, your name will fill the screen or paper.

✧ When this happens, say:
So shall my business grow and prosper and increase.
As I write, it shall be so.

✧ Print out the largest name or use the last piece of paper you wrote on, and pin it behind the door of your workspace, so you can see it as you work. If you hit problems, write your name again very large and repeat:
So shall my business grow and prosper and increase.
As I write, it shall be so.

A spell so that a major project or deal will succeed

Whether you are working for yourself or a multi national, you may suddenly find you have to organise a major project, increase orders, negotiate a deal or train other people. You may have to deal with other people who may be unwilling to co-operate or change their working practices. This spell will give you the initial impetus to launch and the drive to carry the project to successful completion.

You will need: A stream, a lake or river with a bridge and five blue flowers.

Best time: If possible when the Sun and Moon are both in the sky, the Sun moving towards setting in the West, the Moon rising in the East. On the days just before full Moon you can see quite a sizeable lunar disk if the sky is clear. Use *Old Moore's Almanack* or the weather chapter in the paper to co-ordinate times.

The spell

✧ Stand on the bridge holding your five flowers. Raise them first to the Sun and then to the Moon, saying:
Moon power, Sun power, at this hour, Moon power, Sun power, fill each flower, that I may shine.

✧ Take the first flower and name what it represents, either a quality you need, such as leadership, an approach you need to adopt or a step you need to take in fulfilling the project. Do not think beforehand what you are going to say, but allow your unconscious wisdom to speak. It may cast up new issues and inspiration.

✧ Cast the flower from the bridge upstream, saying:
Grow as the river, flow to the sea, fulfil my venture, successfully.

✧ As you did when you were a child, watch your wish sail under the bridge and off downstream.

✧ Continue until you have launched all five wishes.

✧ If any get caught in the bank, try to rescue them. If you fail, this may be a good indicator that the aspect you named for that flower needs special care or that the strength or approach is not the right one.

✧ If all get caught or sink, repeat the spell another day until they do sail away. (Don't make it hard for yourself by choosing a weed-choked stream.)

A spell for recovering from redundancy or unfair dismissal

There can be all kinds of reasons for things going wrong at work: the malice of a colleague, an insecure boss, a slump in orders or a major take-over. The worst aspect, even if you are given more than the minimum redundancy or win at a tribunal, is the destruction of self-belief, the niggling fear that we were somehow to blame.

I have recently faced major problems brought about by forced redundancy and unfair dismissal within my family and know the heartache as well as the financial struggles it brings. Alongside earthly efforts, magic can help to overcome the fear of failure and self-defeat at a time when we need every bit of willpower and confidence to climb back. The spell is also good, as I found, for the relations of the victims as they can suffer too, but need to keep up a confident, encouraging appearance, even when they are panicking inside.

You will need: A plot of damp earth (you can water it if necessary beforehand), thick-soled shoes or boots, a deep plant pot, a spade and some fast-growing herbs or flowers. You can plant any of the career herbs listed (see pages 119–120) or choose a personal favourite (thyme works especially well).

Best time: Early morning.

The spell

◇ Stand in the soil with your legs apart and press down with your feet until both feet have made an impression in the soil. Say:

I am myself, I am complete, failure is earth beneath my feet.

◇ Repeat this three times and really stamp your impression.

◇ Now walk around the plot of earth in an anticlockwise direction. Stamp hard as you walk, leaving footprints and saying:

Out with anger, out with pain, I am myself, myself remain.

◇ Then reverse your direction and continue to stamp until the area is filled with your mingled footprints. This time, as you tread, say:

I am myself, I make my mark. I will fight back, though all seems dark.

◇ With the spade, fill the plant pot with your footprints and plant the herbs or flowers, saying:

From dark to light, grow to great height, so I shall rise and touch the skies.

◇ Keep your plant where it gets plenty of light and repeat the words of the spell over the plant whenever you become despondent.

A spell for coping with new technology or learning new skills at work

A job we have been doing for years may suddenly change, perhaps because of a take-over or because the firm has bought a new computer system. Or you may need to learn new skills to run your business from home. Especially as we get older, some of us, myself included, panic at the sight of unfamiliar scanners, upgraded word processing systems and design programmes. I freeze at the sight of a manual and my brain turns to jelly. This is where a few magical energies can open the channels necessary for change – which may prove a blessing and timesaver.

This spell calls on Mercury, the Roman god of learning and more recently a symbol of technological wizardry.

You will need: Any manual, book or paperwork connected with the new process, a small purse, small quantities of any of the memory-enhancing herbs, dried parsley, sage, rosemary or thyme (see also page 137), a mortar and pestle or deep dish and wooden spoon, and three yellow candles.

Best time: Before bed, on one of the nights around the full Moon if possible.

The spell
✧ Position the mortar and pestle with the herbs in it, the purse and the manual in the centre of the table. Arrange the yellow candles in a triangle around these items.

✧ Light the candles and take the manual out of the triangle. Open it anywhere and read a few lines aloud. Say:
Parsley, sage, rosemary, thyme, by the power of Mercury, make this knowledge mine.

✧ Return the book to the centre and next take the mortar and pestle or bowl and spoon out of the triangle of candles.

✧ Grind the herbs with the pestle or spoon, faster and faster, chanting:
Parsley, sage, rosemary, thyme, by the power of Mercury, make this knowledge mine.

✧ When you can't chant any faster, plunge the pestle or spoon down in the bowl with a final:
Knowledge is mine.

✧ Scatter a circle of herbs clockwise round the outside of the triangle of candles. Then scatter a second circle around this and finally a third circle to enclose both the triangle and the other two circles. As you do this, say:
Enter the pages, clear to see, fixed within these circles three.

✧ Blow out the three candles. In your mind, direct the light into the book so that it will become clear.

✧ Place the manual next to your bed and when you wake read the same lines again.

Chapter 9

Spells for Learning New Skills and Passing Tests and Examinations

If you have children you will know how hard it can be to get them to settle to homework or to revise for examinations. In our own lives too, we may have to take tests, attend formal interviews or update skills. In most cases problems arise not through lack of ability, but lack of confidence. Children too may not want to go to school because some subject or skill is difficult and the more anxious they become, the more they block their ability to learn.

Whether struggling to put together so-called self-assembly furniture or to begin a first novel, we may need to focus and channel our natural powers and talents into a specific project. Spells can not only break down our natural barriers to learning but can create around us positive vibes that enable us to sail through a driving test or major interview just because our natural competence shines through.

Learning spell correspondences

Candles: Blue for formal knowledge, examinations and tests of all kinds; yellow for increased memory, concentration and technological expertise, also for learning healing and alternative medical practices; brown for practical skills.

Incenses and oils: Eucalyptus, fennel and tea tree for learning new skills and technical expertise; frankincense for formal or long-term acquisition of knowledge; parsley, rosemary, sage and thyme for increased memory and concentration; sandalwood and pine for healing wisdom.

Crystals: Amazonite, carnelian and laboradite for confidence; citrine, quartz crystals, falcon's eye and haematite for focus, concentration and learning new skills; amber, desert rose and lapis lazuli for formal knowledge.

Best time: Wednesday is best for mastering new technology and when there is only a short time available for learning. Thursday is good for longer-term study.

A spell for revising for examinations and for improving concentration

This is a good spell, especially for teenagers, as you can add the empowered herbs to evening meals. Parsley, sage, rosemary and thyme are the traditional herbs of good memory and concentration. At one time people would wear a sprig of sage in their hats or place thyme beneath the pillow to aid learning.

Knots too are linked with memory, and people used to tie a knot in their handkerchief to remind them of something they had to do during the day. Each time they took out the handkerchief they were reminded. In the modern world where disposable tissues have all but replaced the handkerchief, we have to rely on bleeping personal organisers.

You will need: A small quantity of parsley, sage, rosemary and thyme. You can use dried culinary herbs. Also a mortar and pestle or bowl and wooden spoon, a square of yellow cloth and some yellow twine or cord.

Best time: If possible on the waxing Moon, early mornings are best.

The spell

✧ Place the four herbs together in the bowl or mortar. Mix with a spoon or pestle, while chanting faster and faster as you stir faster and faster to empower the herbs:
  Parsley, sage, rosemary, thyme, as I stir and mix these herbs, make memory mine.

✧ When you can chant no faster, call:
  The power is free so shall it be. Memory is mine, by parsley, sage, rosemary, thyme.

✧ Scoop a little of the empowered herbs into a sealed tub to use in cooking.

✧ Tie the rest in the square of yellow cloth, securing the cord round it with three knots, while saying:

Three, two, one, the spell is done. One, two, three, the power's in me/(the person for whom the spell is done).

✧ Hide the herb sachet where the teenager works or, if you have carried out the spell for yourself, keep it in your study space.

A spell for passing a driving test

This is a spell I am frequently asked to carry out on behalf of other people, since nervousness in a test situation can be the downfall of many competent, would-be successful drivers. The spell not only calms nerves, but also attracts good fortune, perhaps in the form of good driving conditions or an examiner who has just learned of a small lottery win or met the partner of his or her dreams.

You will need: A map that includes the area in which the test will take place, a toy car, four yellow candles with holders and a rosemary or sage incense stick. An amazonite or carnelian crystal is optional and can be empowered during the spell as a talisman.

Best time: If someone close to you is taking the test you can carry out the spell just before the time of the test. For yourself, work the evening before the day of the test.

The spell

✧ Using deep holders so that the wax does not drip on to the map, position the four candles around the edges of the map, about half-way along each side facing approximately North, East, South and West. Light the candles.

❖ Set the toy car in the place on the map where the test will begin.

❖ Using the North-facing candle, light the incense or smudge stick, saying:

North, South, East, West, let me/(name of person) pass the driving test.

❖ Repeat the chant over the other three candles, holding the incense stick so that it briefly touches each flame as you speak the chant again.

❖ Finally, in the air over the toy car, write in smoke 'Pass'.

❖ If you want to empower a crystal you can set it next to the car at the beginning of the spell and then carry it with you to the test.

❖ Leave the candles to burn down.

A spell for learning another language

Whether we need to learn another language for business purposes or so that we can enjoy foreign holidays more or even to start a new life abroad on retirement, it can be difficult to attune the ear and voice to different speech rhythms once we have left school. The following spell takes advantage of our ability to absorb information unconsciously as well as consciously. After the spell you will still need to follow a language course, but it will be so much easier because your unconscious mind will have sown the seeds.

You will need: A picture of people in the country whose

language you wish to learn (it can be a photograph, a downloaded and printed image from the Internet or one taken from a holiday brochure). Also a CD or tape recording of the language and a portable player you can set by your bed.

Best time: Just before you go to sleep on two or three consecutive nights. The early waxing Moon phase can ease the learning.

The spell

✧ Put the CD or tape ready in the player so you just have to switch it on.

✧ Sit up in bed with the light on and, holding the picture between your hands, memorise the details. If you have been to the country already you can add memories of fragrances, intense heat or cool rain.

✧ Turn off the light and set the picture on your bedside table.

✧ Lie in the darkness and visualise the scene as vividly as you can. Recite softly the customary greeting of the country you are going to visit. I have chosen the Swedish 'Hej', which means hello and is pronounced hay. Then create a rhyme round it. The one I have used works for a number of languages.

Hej, I greet you. Hej, I meet you. I speak to you, you speak to me, hej, hej, hej.

✧ Turn on the CD or tape very low so you can hardly hear it and drift off to sleep carried by the gentle sound, and still holding the scene in your mind.

✧ When you listen to the CD during waking hours, begin by
reciting the rhyme and looking at the picture once more.

A four-day spell for mastering new technology

Whether you are experienced with computers or, like me, know
what to do as long as everything keeps working, technological
skills are now part of many jobs as well as an aid to leisure. The
Internet holds a whole world of information that, once
accessed, is like having your own library and museum in the
living room.

But it can be daunting, especially if a familiar job is suddenly
changed to one dependent on learning a whole new technical
system. In such a case the computer or audio-visual equipment
manual seems to take on a life of its own and to bear absolutely
no resemblance to the machine in front of you. Panic sets in,
which blocks our innate adaptability and problem-solving
abilities. Spells help in two ways, by overcoming these blocks
and by helping us to absorb new information rapidly and easily
by increasing focus and concentration.

You will need: Your computer manual or a book explaining
the new form of technology, ten incense sticks of fennel,
rosemary or frankincense, each in its own holder, a ceramic
bowl of water.

Best time: On the three days before and the day of the full
Moon, or four days around the full Moon, or four consecutive
days. The spell is best carried out close to noon.

The spell

✧ Place your manual on a table. Open it either at a chapter that is worrying you or at the beginning if you have found the topic too daunting to make a start.

✧ Place four incense sticks in deep holders around the manual. These should be positioned at the centre of each side of the book and at approximately the four main directions. You may need to move the book a little to do this.

✧ Place the bowl of water on another table nearby.

✧ On the first day, light the four incense sticks, beginning with the one in the North and continuing in a clockwise direction. As you do this, say:

One brings knowledge, two understanding, three enlightenment, four success. I will succeed.

✧ Take the incense stick in the North from its holder and plunge it into the water, saying:

So I remove one barrier to understanding.

✧ Leave the other sticks to burn down. Meanwhile read the opening chapter or your chosen chapter of the manual straight through without stopping and then try it out in practice, if possible. If you still do not know what you are doing, do not worry, as there are three more days of the spell to go. Dispose of the used incense sticks and replace the water.

✧ On the second night, open the manual at the next chapter or at another chapter that is causing you concern.

✧ Light three new incense sticks in the East, South and West, saying:

Two brings understanding, three enlightenment, four success. I will succeed.

✧ Take the incense stick in the East and plunge it into the water, saying:

So I remove one barrier to understanding.

✧ Leave the other sticks to burn down. Read the chapter that you have chosen and, if possible, apply it without worrying. Dispose of the extinguished incense and put fresh water in the bowl.

✧ On the third night, open the manual at the next chapter or at another chapter of your choice.

✧ Light two new incense sticks, one to the South and one to the West of the manual and say:

Three brings enlightenment, four success. I will succeed.

✧ Take the incense in the South and plunge it into the water, saying:

So I remove one barrier to understanding.

✧ Again leave the remaining incense to burn while you read the manual and try out the instructions in practice, if possible.

✧ Dispose of the used incense and change the water.

✧ On the fourth night, choose another chapter and light only the incense in the West, saying:

Four brings success. I will succeed.

✧ Take the final incense and extinguish it the water, saying:
  I remove the final barrier and claim success.
✧ Read and apply this chapter of the manual and dispose of the used incense, washing out the bowl.
✧ When you get worried in future, sit calmly in front of the equipment you are trying to master, close your eyes and say in your mind:
  One brings knowledge, two understanding, three enlightenment, four success. I claim success.

A spell for beginning study or retraining later in life

The University of the Third Age is a very popular concept which involves people approaching retirement beginning to study in a way that was not possible when they were busy with jobs or families. Others choose to take examinations or study for a college degree many years after leaving school, as I did, or go to evening classes after work. Redundancy or a change of career can also involve formal learning long after school days have ended.

I found that studying later in life was in some ways easier than at school because I had so much more focus, and the timetable of fitting in study with bringing up children prevented me frittering away precious study time. But I did nearly give up several times through tiredness.

The following spell is good for getting started and, if repeated periodically whenever determination wavers, helps to refocus your determination.

You will need: A kite or helium balloon, a paper luggage tag or strip of sticky backed paper and a pen.

Best time: Any windy day, if possible during the period of the waxing Moon.

The spell

✧ Go to an open place, preferably the top of a hill. You will feel your kite or balloon tugging to be free.

✧ Tie it securely to a tree or post while you write the achievement or qualification you want on the label. You can either make a wish to get through the first part of the course or to achieve the desired results for the whole training or retraining.

✧ Tie or stick the label to the balloon or kite and hold the label in your power hand (with the kite string in the other).

✧ Launch your venture by releasing the balloon, saying:
   Fly from me, high from me, skywards be, as you carry my wishes into the world.

✧ Run or walk down the hill or across the plain with your arms wide, so that the wind billows through your clothes and you are filled with energy and enthusiasm for your new venture.

A spell for developing creative powers

We all have creative gifts, whether for cookery, arts and crafts, writing or painting to name but a few. Sometimes this skill is discovered at school, but as we become immersed in work and family, we may put it aside. Then, suddenly, years later we may feel the desire to write a novel, set up a new career as a photographer, grow beautiful flowers or create beautiful meals and maybe write a recipe book or sell recipes online. I did not write my first book until I was forty and now, fourteen years later, I have had almost fifty titles published.

This spell will help you to make the most of your creative powers.

You will need: The tools or ingredients for your chosen activity, a long, thin roll of paper, a pen and a thin, yellow cord or ribbon.

Best time: When you first see the crescent Moon in the sky, if possible.

The spell

✧ Gather together everything you will need to begin work and set it where you can sit facing the ingredients or tools and see the Moon through a window beyond. Forget superstitions about seeing the Moon through glass.

✧ Write on the roll of paper your declaration of intention, as a single phrase or short sentence, and your chosen time scale. This can be as ambitious or modest as you wish, for example,

147

bake and decorate a Christmas cake by the weekend, write a song by Sunday, finish a novel by Christmas. Say the words out loud as you write.

◇ Keep writing and reciting the same words in a continuous line, leaving no spaces between the words. Write and recite faster and faster until you can feel the enthusiasm and intensity of purpose building up in you.

◇ When you have filled the roll or reached the peak of intensity, call out:
   The spell is done as I count one. Moon, be my witness.

◇ Roll up the paper and tie it with the cord, using a single knot. Keep this in your workspace. While still facing the Moon, begin work.

A spell for learning or improving practical skills such as DIY or car maintenance

Those of us who are not gifted with practical skills have probably experienced the sheer panic of trying to assemble a wardrobe from a kit and finding the crucial part has been fixed upside down. Or you may wait for the breakdown service for hours on a cold, wet night, only to discover the problem with the car was a simple loose connection. There are many good books available on DIY and car maintenance, but to get us going, a spell is a good way of rekindling our innate survival instincts to create our own shelter (or at least one for clothes) and to journey under our own steam. If you are slightly clumsy, as I am, the spell can also kick-start the parts of the brain that fine-tune our hand-to-eye co-ordination. For those with basic know-how, this spell can develop increased expertise.

You will need: Six shiny new nails or screws (six being the number of balance and harmony), a dish of salt, a small patch of flower bed with soft soil or a deep tray or pot of earth, a ready-growing herb such as fennel, rosemary or sage in a small pot.

Best time: The morning before undertaking a practical project.

The spell

✧ Either take your nails out to the flower bed or sit with them beside your tray of earth indoors.

✧ Draw a large circle in the earth and then position the nails, sharp point inwards, around the circle. Say:
So I return metal to soil, that I may toil, with skill and with dexterity.

✧ Plant the herb in the centre of the circle, using your hands so that your fingers become dirty. Say:
Grow and seed, your power I need, to make and mend. Send to me the gift of (name the area of expertise you want).

✧ Now push each nail deep into the soil. The nails should still be in a circle but should not touch the roots of the plant. As you do this, say:
Bed deep into the earth, bring craftsmanship to birth. As it shall grow, so I shall show, my new-found skill. This I ask. It shall be so.

A spell for overcoming panic when learning a new or difficult skill

This spell is suitable for adults and children as both can experience fear when faced with learning something new. Children can become very anxious about acquiring a new skill, especially if they are naturally shy or have experienced teasing. For some, the idea even of a simple test can make them physically sick or cause them to under-achieve.

Adults too can experience the same feelings when they are suddenly thrust into the limelight or have to master a skill such as swimming or cycling that they missed learning in childhood.

Jade is probably the best anti-panic crystal, but instead of making the crystal into an amulet and taking it to the feared event or training session, you are going to transfer the fears to it and then leave the crystal and the fears behind.

You will need: A jade or rose quartz crystal small enough to fit in the palm of your hand, some cotton wool and a box or drawstring bag.

Best time: Any time during the waning Moon cycle at twilight, but any twilight if the need is urgent.

The spell

✧ Work in a quiet place indoors or outdoors. Ask the child to hold the jade crystal in their receptive hand (not the one they write with) and to cover the crystal with the other hand.

✧ If the child is young or very frightened, you can enclose his or her hands within yours. If your child is self-conscious, demonstrate the spell with one of your own learning fears.

✧ Let the child talk of his or her fears and doubts. You can then describe these fears entering the crystal and leaving the child through green rays of light. With your own fears, describe them aloud as though talking to a friend.

✧ Explain to the child that the crystal may start to feel heavy.

✧ When the child is finished, say softly:
It is gone, it is done. Peace come.

✧ Help the child to wrap the jade in cotton wool and put it in the box or bag. Repeat:
It is gone, it is done. Peace come.

✧ Let the child hide the crystal where only he or she knows the location.

✧ You may need to repeat the spell a number of times and hide a number of crystals before the child gains in confidence.

✧ If you are working with your own private fear of learning, hide the box in the darkest place you can find.

Chapter 10
Travel and Holiday Spells

Travel, especially for holidays, is exciting and it is now possible to visit even exotic locations for a long weekend. But as we travel more, so can the hazards increase. As traffic becomes heavier, both on the roads and in the skies, delays and dangers can become more acute.

Terrorist attacks have also made some people, even those who previously enjoyed flying, more apprehensive. Other perils can occur in the course of daily commuting: being alone on a station late at night when a train has been cancelled or waiting for a pre-booked mini cab that fails to turn up.

The spells in this chapter won't make motorway jams miraculously disappear or solve an air traffic control problem. However, they will help us to flow more harmoniously with the natural energies so that we not only instinctively avoid hazards, but also enjoy to the full those precious times away from work.

Travel spell correspondences

Candles: Yellow for short-haul journeys, mini-holidays and air travel; blue for long-distance travel, long-duration stays and commuting; silver for journeys across water and for protection while travelling.

Incenses and oils: Basil, fennel and sage for protection while travelling; fern, frankincense and pine for all holiday spells; lavender and mint for trouble-free journeys and harmonious holidays.

Crystals: Amethyst, jet, smoky quartz, garnet or bloodstone for general protection while travelling and on holiday; sodalite for air travel; moonstone for travel by night; aquamarine for protection on the sea and when travelling overseas; turquoise to prevent accidents or attack while travelling. Turquoise is particularly good for animals in transit and for safe horse riding.

Best time: Tuesday is a good day for travel spells.

A general travel spell

Whenever you embark on a journey, you hope that there won't be traffic jams or diversions, that trains will turn up approximately on time, that there will not be delays at the airport or ferry port. Whether it is a journey for work or pleasure, a long holiday, a weekend break or regular commuting, you want it all to go smoothly so that you arrive rested and ready for fun or work.

You will need: Basic ingredients to make pastry or dough (110 g/4 oz flour, 50 g/2 oz fat, water to mix), a bowl, a rolling pin, salt, small clear glass nuggets and a jar of dried mint.

Best time: Afternoons with sunshine if possible. It can be useful to cast the spell every few weeks to aid smooth commuting as well as before major trips.

The spell

✧ Add three pinches of salt to the empty mixing bowl and turn the bowl three times clockwise for each pinch, saying:
 Salt clear the pathway, three times three, that I may travel easily.

✧ Add all the ingredients to the bowl, stir and knead them, saying over and over as a mantra:
 Smooth my journeys, swift and sure, this spell once cast, long may endure.

✧ Roll out a long, thin strip of pastry or dough to represent the unfolding pathway, then make it into a circle to symbolise travelling there and back. As you work, visualise the journey unwinding smoothly before you.

✧ All round the pastry path sprinkle mint, saying:
 Travel safe and reach the end, calm upon my road to send, smooth my pathways, safe and sure, this spell once cast, long may endure.

✧ Finally press glass nuggets along the circuit, seeing each as a major potential hazard or stopping point overcome and saying for each:
 The road is light, the path is clear, my journey safe, and without fear.

✧ Leave the pastry till dusk and then roll it with the nuggets and mint into a ball. Bury it beneath a living tree.

A spell for getting the holiday you want

We all have dreams of visiting certain places, and sometimes opportunities do arise to fulfil these dreams. The local travel agent may have a last-minute holiday that they cannot sell or a friend or relation may move to the area or country you want to visit and offer you cheap accommodation. What a spell can do is to bring the desired location into your personal sphere of possibility and open up alternative ways of attaining your dream.

You will need: Four fern or frankincense incense sticks in holders. Use broad-based holders so you can safely place them on top of a map. You will also require a small toy or model to represent the mode of travel and a map that includes the place to which you hope to travel and your present location.

Best time: During the waxing Moon period, or dawn on any day.

The spell

✧ Set the map on a table and surround it with four incense sticks, one at each of the symbolic main directions.

✧ Place the desired mode of transport half-way between you and your ideal holiday location. Make sure the toy car, train, plane or boat is facing in the right direction.

✧ Light the incense sticks, beginning with the one nearest your home and then following round clockwise. For each stick, say:

I span the globe instantly and blow away successfully all barriers to my journey to (name of place).

✧ Take the first incense stick you lit and pass it round the outside of the map saying:
Power of Air carry me, to where it is I wish to be.

✧ Next pass the incense in a direct line from your present home to the desired destination, pausing at regular intervals to make smoke circles enclosing the visualised line at various points. As you do this, repeat:
Power of Air carry me, to where it is I wish to be.

✧ Place the first incense stick in its holder just next to your desired destination and repeat the words and actions with the other three incense sticks until all four make a tight square around your chosen place.

✧ Finally pick up the toy mode of transport and set it in this square, saying:
Carry me by land and sea, to where it is I wish to be.

✧ Leave the incense to burn down while you close your eyes and visualise yourself as clearly as possible holidaying or even living temporarily in the chosen location, evoking sounds and fragrances as well as images.

A spell for a safe journey and holiday

If you are travelling a long way or on an unfamiliar route or one of your family members is going away, you can carry out a spell to enfold either yourself or them in protection. This can be reassuring if a child is going on a school trip or leaving for college for the first time. The spell is also protective against road rage.

You will need: A St Christopher medallion or one of the protective travel crystals (see page 153). Moonstones and turquoise are especially potent. Also three silver candles, a silver ribbon and a tiny drawstring bag or purse.

Best time: The night before travel after dusk.

The spell

✧ Arrange the candles in a triangle. This formation is very protective but also empowering.

✧ Set the St Christopher medallion or protective crystal in the centre of the triangle on top of the purse or bag.

✧ Light the candles, beginning with the single one at the top, saying for each:
   Protective light, keep me/my child/friend safe upon this journey. Guardian angels three, stand sentinel and let no harm befall me/him/her.

✧ Pass the St Christopher or crystal over each of the three candles in turn, saying:
   Light enter this amulet and keep me/him/her safe from weather, harm and danger, thoughtless friend or angry stranger and bring me/him/her safely home again.

✧ Place the St Christopher or crystal inside the purse or bag and bind it with the ribbon. Tie three knots in the ribbon and say:

> *Bind against malice and malevolence, accident and injury,*
> *by the power of three, blessed be this token.*

✧ Leave the candles to burn down while you make quiet preparations.

✧ Place the purse either in the luggage or in the glove compartment of the car.

A spell for enjoying travelling and holidaying alone

With an increase in divorce and people choosing to live alone, a growing number of people holiday by themselves. Those with families may also welcome short solitary breaks to recharge their batteries. But it is natural to feel nervous, especially if the trip is not an organised one.

Although I have travelled extensively in different countries, when I arrive in an unfamiliar town or country, I still feel momentary panic, especially if I do not speak the language. Recalling a few lines of this spell helps me to take charge and transforms the experience into an adventure.

The knights of old would put on their silver armour as they rode off alone in search of dragons or maidens to be rescued and you too can use silver to protect you on your travels. What's more, they rarely came home without an amorous adventure or three (though, of course, that is optional).

You will need: Four small wall mirrors, a white or glittery cloth, six silver candles, a clear quartz crystal and three fern or frankincense incense sticks.

Best time: Any time before travel, though waxing Moon influences are always helpful for spells of increase. Work at sunrise.

The spell

✧ Push all furniture against the wall or take it out of the room.

✧ Arrange your mirrors on four walls and, in the centre of the room, either set a table covered with a white or glittery cloth or spread the cloth on the floor.

✧ Set the candles in a square on the cloth with the quartz crystal in the centre and the incense sticks in a row behind the crystal and inside the candles, so they face you.

✧ Kneel or sit on the floor outside the square of candles or sit at the table.

✧ Light the candles, saying for each:
I am myself, in unity, body, mind and spirit free.

✧ Light the incense from left to right, saying:
Body, mind and spirit free, happiness is within me.

✧ Holding the crystal in your power hand (the one you write with), stand up and swirl round nine times, so your reflection spirals in the mirrors, and the crystal makes mini-rainbows. Repeat the chant:
Happiness within me lies, in my heart and in my eyes, in my body and my mind, joy in light around I bind, bind within,

above, below. The spell is done, let it be so.
✧ Extinguish each of the candles in reverse order, chanting:
   Four, three, two, one, I greet the Sun.
✧ Take the crystal on holiday with you and set it in your hotel
   room or room where you are staying.

A spell when unexpected danger looms while travelling

Even the best planned trips or journeys can go wrong and you
may find yourself lost in an undesirable area of a foreign city or
in a situation in which you are not comfortable. You can carry
out this spell in advance and then recall it at the moment of
danger or insecurity. It may be helpful to renew it every few
months. Just as in the money chapter we increased our money-
attracting aura, so you can lower your psychic profile in order
to move around relatively unnoticed and without giving off
natural anxiety vibes that can identify you as a potential victim.

You will need: A sage smudge stick or a lavender or sage
incense stick. Use a broad, long incense stick that you can hold
easily and will not crumble.

Best time: Initially during the period of the waning Moon, at
twilight if possible. Alternatively any twilight.

The spell
✧ Work in the open air if you can. Extend your arms as far as
   you can above your head, to the sides and sweep down to the

floor. This is the extent of the average aura or psychic energy field, which surrounds us all and connects us with other people.

✧ Light your smudge or incense stick and, in traditional style, face the four directions in turn, beginning with the North, extending the smudge stick in front of you at each direction. As you face the North, say:

May blessings and protection surround and enclose me, wise guardians of the North. So shall it be.

✧ Adapt the words for the other three directions.

✧ When you have done this, point the smoking smudge stick to the ground, saying:

May blessings and protection surround and enclose me, Mother Earth.

✧ Finally, point to the sky, saying:

May blessings and protection surround and enclose me, Father Sky.

✧ Now you are going to cast a cloak of invisibility round yourself. Beginning at ground level and in front of your body, swirl the smudge or incense stick upwards from side to side, over your head and around your back. As you swirl, move rhythmically so that your aura's energy field blends with the smoke. Chant:

Grey of smoke, hide sight of me, from those who come in enmity. Let me fade and disappear, that my foes may come not near.

✧ Make a sign that will call up the grey aura instantly when you are in need of protection. You could make a cross in the palm of your hand or place your right hand on your heart. While you are making your chosen sign, say:
When I make this sign, I will draw round me my cloak of invisibility.

✧ When you have finished, leave the smudge to burn in a holder and sit quietly, allowing yourself to flow into the twilight.

✧ Switch on the light and shake yourself like a dog, right down to your fingers and toes, to restore the natural brightness to your aura.

✧ Whenever you feel in need of protection, make your chosen sign.

A spell for a happy holiday

Whether we are going away for a weekend or a month, we can experience anxiety as well as anticipation. Will the accommodation be nice? Will the weather be fine and will the different members of the family or friends mix together harmoniously?

A spell that can be activated every morning is a good way of releasing positive vibes so that any unavoidable setbacks can become part of the fun and not a damper on the holiday, and any potential conflicts caused by different generations or personalities will melt away.

You will need: Four green candles, a long, green cord (associated with love and friendship, as well as travel), and four gentle travel incense sticks (for example lavender) in holders.

Best time: The day before your holiday, in the morning if possible.

The spell

✧ Position the four candles at the main direction points. Then place the incense sticks equidistant between them in a circle.

✧ Place the cord in the centre.

✧ Light each of the candles in turn beginning with the one in the North and moving in a clockwise direction, saying:
Light of laughter, travel with me, over land and over sea, light of love and harmony. This I ask and it shall be.

✧ Light the incense sticks, beginning with the one in the North East, saying:
Breath of kindness, travel with me, over land and over sea, bringing joy and unity. This I ask and it shall be.

✧ Pass the cord across the candle in the North so it singes but does not flare up, and say:
Seal in hope for happy days, sunshine and tranquillity, pleasure in so many ways. This I ask and it shall be.

✧ Pass the cord through the smoke of the incense in the South West, saying:
Happiness in fullest measure, memories to always treasure, joined in harmony are we. This I ask and it shall be.

✧ Tie knots in the cord, one for every day of the holiday. The last knot will be formed when the cord is joined at the ends. As you tie each, make a wish or empowerment for what you want from the holiday for yourself and for those who are sharing the time with you. End each wish with:
This I ask and it shall be.

✧ Take the cord with you in your luggage. Undo a knot every morning of your holiday, starting with the knot that joins the end of the cord on the morning that you travel. Make a wish for a happy day as you untie each knot.

A spell for overcoming children's travel sickness

A spell to help prevent car, air or boat sickness is high on my list of priorities as it is a problem that can make even the simplest journey a nightmare. It can be helpful if the child shares the ritual. The spell can also help motion-queasy adults.

You will need: Dried lavender and mint (the kind you use in cooking is fine), a few drops of rose essential oil, rose essence or perfumed rose water and a mortar and pestle or a bowl and wooden spoon. Also a small, featureless bear made out of two pieces of cloth sewn together with purple thread (leave a few stitches around the head to be finished so that there is room to add the herbs during the spell).

Best time: The waning Moon is best, but any time as dusk falls is suitable.

The spell

✧ Take the herbs and dried lavender and place them in the bowl or mortar. If the child is old enough, allow him or her to stir the mixture, getting faster and faster, while you both repeat nine times:
  Lavender, mint, drive away sickness from the car/plane/boat this day. Mint and lavender set me free, so I can travel happily.

✧ After the final 'happily', the child can add three drops of rose oil or rose water, naming for each drop a favourite destination. While stirring in the oil he or she can say with you:
  As I count now to three, so sickness you must flee. One, two, three, so shall it be. Three, two, one, sickness is gone.

✧ Add the empowered herbs to the cut-out bear shape. As the child spoons in the herbs, he or she can say with you:
  I fill this bear with peace and joy. Keep me safe, my little toy.

✧ Sew the final stitches, adding a wish, with each stitch, for happy journeys and all the good things that can happen as a result of travelling: seeing grandma, going to the sea, stopping at a favourite motorway café.

✧ At the beginning of the next journey give the bear to the child or hang it up over the car seat if the child is very small and might chew it.

✧ If you are in a hurry or want to prevent adult nausea, substitute a small purse to hold the herbs, modifying the words accordingly.

A spell for overcoming fear of flying

Even people who do not have a phobia about flying can be very apprehensive about take off and landing, and the hijackings in America have left even experienced flyers feeling jittery.

You will need: A small, wide-necked, dark, plastic bottle with a lid, still mineral water, a small sodalite crystal or some other dark crystal (such as a deep amethyst), dried basil or a growing basil plant (basil is very good for overcoming fears of flying) and a small, deep blue cloth or flannel.

Best time: The evening before travelling. You can repeat part of the spell when you are in the aircraft.

The spell

✧ Half fill the bottle with still mineral water and add your sodalite or dark crystal.

✧ Surround the bottle with a circle of basil, and say:
   Through the sky, plane fly, fear do not remain. Fly high through the sky, land smooth, fear remove.

✧ Leave the crystal in the water until the morning, then remove it and put the lid on the bottle.

✧ When you travel, slip your crystal into your hand luggage along with the bottle of water and flannel. Just before take off, moisten the flannel with the water and rub it on your temples and wrists, while reciting the spell in your mind.

✧ Repeat this process if you encounter any turbulence and before landing. Empower some more water before you return.

Chapter 11
Spells for Animals

Like children, pets are highly intuitive. Domestic animals routinely wait in the hall five minutes before their owners return, even though the time may vary by hours. Animals will bark or hiss at a stranger who is not trustworthy. Because they are so open, animals are receptive to spells, especially those for healing and protection and so they need only very simple rituals.

As we become increasingly aware of the problems of deforestation and pollution of wildlife habitats, so a number of people, myself included, are beginning to understand the importance of sending regular healing and protection to creatures in the wild, especially those species that are endangered in the modern world.

Take particular care to keep candles well away from where animals can knock them over and as animals tend not to like burning materials, use a diffuser for oils in animal spells. Animals have a special affinity with crystals, whether they are used to send healing light to a sick animal or are circled over the creature to bring calm.

Animal spell correspondences

Candles: Pink for healing; brown for older animals and for protection; green for endangered species and for love between owner and pet.

Incenses and oils: Mint, rosemary, sage and thyme rather than floral fragrances. You can also make use of natural herbs.

Crystals: Earth stones such as brown and banded agates and smoky quartz for protection, soothing hyperactivity and for older animals; golden brown rutilated quartz and jaspers for energising; turquoise, the ultimate animal-protection stone, to prevent an animal straying, being hurt or being stolen. Jade is a multi-purpose crystal, good for gentle energising as well as calming. Jade under a pet bed or placed in water before use can fill an animal with gentle energy or relax a hyperactive pet.

Best time: Saturday is the best day for animal spells.

A spell for finding the right pet

Many people discover a pet quite by chance. We once went to collect a kitten called Archie from the RSPCA, but he was ill and the children were then captivated by a huge, black and white cat, Simba, who began swinging from the bars of his pen. Once home, he never moved from the food bowl.

Before you visit potential pets, carry out the following spell and, as with any lasting love affair, you and your pet will be instinctively drawn together.

You will need: A large mirror, five small green and pink candles or nightlights (three green and two pink) in separate holders.

Best time: The hour after sunset on the day before you begin to look for your pet.

The spell

✧ Arrange the candles with alternate colours in a horseshoe formation. Position the mirror in front of this shape so that the light from the candles reflects in the mirror.

✧ Stand behind the candles looking into the mirror and say:
Friend, I call you now to me, faithful always may you be, in return my care will give, comfort, love while you shall live.

✧ Blow out the candles at each end and send the light to wherever your future pet may be, asking silently that you may recognise each other when you meet.

✧ Look again into the mirror and repeat:
Friend, I call you now to me, faithful always may you be, in return my care will give, comfort, love while you shall live.

✧ Blow out the next two outermost candles, again sending the light to wherever your pet may be, asking the cosmos silently that you will recognise each other.

✧ Look now into the mirror by the light of the single remaining candle and say:
Friend, I call you now to me, faithful always may you be, show yourself that I may see, how you look when you greet me.

✧ Close your eyes, open them, blink and stare hard into the mirror. You will be rewarded either within the mirror itself or in your mind's vision, with a momentary image of your pet.

✧ Blow out the final candle and send love to your animal, silently reaffirming your offer of care and protection.

✧ When you go to choose or collect your pet, look out for any animal that approaches you. You will recognise it from the vision. You may see the creature on the way to where your prospective animal is kept. Sometimes the animal we think we want and the one right for us are very different, so be guided by intuition and the vision.

A spell for calming a noisy or hyperactive pet

There is a trend to call a pet psychologist or resort to medication if an animal is persistently noisy, hyperactive or aggressive to strangers. But usually there is a reason for a pet to be acting in particular way, especially if it came from a rescue centre. If you sit at a quiet moment, stroking the animal, the animal's feelings will come into your mind as words or images. This natural telepathic communication is universal between pets and owners and is the basis of this spell.

You will need: A large, brown stone or crystal to set between you and your pet. It is best if you can find the stone when you take the animal for a walk or near a spot where it sits in the garden.

Best time: Late in the evening when you are both sleepy.

The spell

✦ For a day or two before the spell, put the stone or crystal between you and your pet whenever you are together to absorb your joint psychic vibes.

✦ On the evening of the spell wait till your pet is settled and pick up the stone or crystal. Because it is full of earth energies, the crystal will act as a transmitter and amplifier of your joint psychic energies.

✦ Begin slowly to breathe in the brown light and with the out breath, just as gently, blow the brown light towards the animal.

✦ Continue and you may see a soft, brown glow growing around the animal. Your pet may visibly relax or, if asleep, sigh contentedly.

✦ Now say quietly over and over like a mantra:
Calm, quiet and tranquil be, filled with love and harmony.
Rest and wake in peace.

✦ You may start to feel very sleepy yourself. Leave the crystal or stone near the pet bed or cage overnight and in the morning place it outdoors. Repeat the ritual when necessary.

A spell for keeping your pet from straying or becoming lost or stolen

Traditionally in European society and later in America, New Zealand and Australia, a turquoise crystal was attached to a bird cage or an animal's collar to keep it safe. Three hairs or small feathers were, in addition, plaited or fastened on to wire or a pliant twig and buried safe in the garden to stop the animal leaving accidentally or being stolen.

Combining the two methods and empowering them with a spell offers powerful protection. If your pet is nervous you can use hairs from the brush when it is groomed or wait till the bird moults. This spell is especially good for protecting horses, as is the next spell.

You will need: Three long hairs or feathers from the animal or bird, a small loop of thin wire or a thin, silver ring, a length of thread, a turquoise crystal, a dish of salt and a small bowl of water.

Best time: After dark on a Moonless night.

The spell

✧ Bind or tie the hairs or feathers round the wire or ring to create a complete circle. Secure the hairs tightly with thread.

✧ As you bind them, chant three times:
Bind protection safe within, wind and wrap from theft or loss, that (name of pet) may not stray or unwillingly be led away.

✧ Put the turquoise in the centre of the ring.

✧ Add three pinches of salt to the bowl of water, stirring them in with the index finger of your power hand (the hand you write with), saying three times:
Salt and water, blessed be, create for (name of pet) a sanctuary.

✧ Using your power hand, sprinkle three circles of empowered water drops moving outwards from the ring, saying:
Three by three the power I raise, recalling happy days, peaceful nights, security, thus for ever may it be.

✧ Attach the turquoise to the animal's collar, bridle, bedding or cage. Bury the ring of hair within the boundaries of your home or in a deep pot in an apartment.

A spell for protecting pets from aggression both from humans and animals

As well as becoming lost or being stolen, your pet can come under threat from hostile humans or other larger or fiercer animals. Whether you are dealing with jealous rivals at a horse or dog show or neighbours who hate animals, you may need to cast round your animal an active circle of protection to repel anger or aggression.

You will need: Sparklers (the kind used on firework night) or an electric torch with a beam that can be set to flash on and off continuously. If you cannot obtain either, you can switch the torch on and off rapidly during the spell. Also some of the animal's water or milk in a bowl and some dried mint or rosemary. Do the spell in the animal's absence because of the sparks or flashing lights.

Best time: Late on a Moonless night.

The spell

❖ Work in the open air when it is very dark, using a torch when setting the bowl of water or milk on the ground. It is important that the bowl touches the earth or at least the ground so that the protective earth energies can rise into the water.

❖ Scatter a single anticlockwise circle of mint or rosemary round the bowl, saying:

Spite and anger come not here, cruel humans cause not fear, fierce predators turn away, your claws and jaws here have no sway.

❖ Light either a sparkler or set the torch to continuous flash and move around the bowl and herbs in nine anticlockwise circles, waving the light or sparkler in anticlockwise circles while saying:

Sparks of fire, beams of light, drive all harm from here this night.

❖ After the final circling call out:

Be gone. Your power is none. Do not come again.

❖ Leave the bowl of water or milk in the open air or near a window and give it to your pet in the morning so that he or she can drink the protection.

❖ Repeat the spell at times when your pet is especially vulnerable.

A spell for a healthy and active pet

Even the healthiest pet needs regular psychic as well as physical cleansing, especially if it lives in a town. With older animals, it can be helpful every few weeks to top up their energy levels and to cleanse their aura or psychic energy field of pollutants both physical and emotional.

Birds tend to have a silvery grey or pale blue energy field all around them, while other animals vary through the shades of brown, with pink and sometimes green for pets with strong bonds to humans such as horses and dogs. Cats may have a purple aura as they keep their mystery even at their most domesticated.

Red can indicate pent up aggression or fear and streaks of black suggest exhaustion and pollutants. You can easily see your pet's aura by staring at your pet when he or she is framed against the light. Just close your eyes, open them, blink and you will see either externally or in your mind's vision your pet's aura all around the body extending like waves of light from the fur to a few centimetres distant in the air. If the psychic energy field seems cloudy, dull or dark, you will know it needs cleansing.

You will need: A round, green jade or rutilated quartz for energising and a smoky quartz or brown agate for absorbing pollution and stress from the animal. Make sure the crystals are of similar shape and size.

Best time: Every few weeks when the weather is calm.

The spell

⋄ Take the pet into the open air or, if this is not possible, a ventilated room and wait until he or she is still, preferably sitting or lying down.

⋄ Face the animal with the jade energising crystal in your power hand (the hand you write with) and the smoky quartz in the other one.

⋄ Begin to rotate your hands, the jade clockwise and the smoky quartz anticlockwise in harmony in the space around the animal, following the outline of the creature.

⋄ Work about 4 cm/1½ in from the animal and move slowly so that your pet does not feel threatened or think you are throwing something to retrieve.

⋄ If your pet becomes over-excited or agitated by your movements, take a few steps backwards and rotate the crystals in front of and just above the height of the animal, drawing an outline of the animal in the air.

⋄ As you work, say:
Go away, flow away, tiredness and illness. Grime of pollution, with each revolution, is replaced by health and vitality.

⋄ Continue to chant and move until the receptive crystal feels heavy. Stop, close your eyes, open them, blink and you will see the circle of energy surrounding your pet is clearer, brighter and lighter than before.

⋄ At this point, raise the crystals to the sky and then lower them to the earth and say:

The spell is done, strength has come. Blessings be on you, my beloved creature.

✧ Wash the crystals under running water and put them together beneath the pet bed overnight to finish their work.

✧ Keep the crystals for this special spell.

A healing spell for pets

If an animal has been unwell or has had an operation, you may need to precede the above spell with this one in order to trigger the creature's own immune system and self-healing powers. This is an adaptation of a spell I have used many times, and is one that again uses the channel of the psychic connection between you and the animal.

You will need: A single earth crystal, such as a banded brown and pink agate. Some of these stones are like earth rainbows. Take your time in choosing one that you will use regularly for your pet.

Best time: When the dawn floods the sky and the world is quiet.

The spell

✧ Facing the direction of the rising Sun, sit or kneel on the ground in front of the animal.

✧ Hold the crystal in your open cupped hands as you rest them over your heart. The heart is a powerful transmitter of higher healing energies from the cosmos and is a major psychic energy centre that controls the smaller energy centres in the palms of your hands.

✧ Say:
Light of the healing morning, shine and give power to this crystal. Light of the morning, flow into my heart.

✧ Set the crystal on the ground between you and the animal and slowly touching first the crystal, then your heart, three or four times until you can feel love flowing like warm liquid in your fingers, place your hands palm down close to the wound or pain on the creature.

✧ If your pet is generally ill or does not wish to be touched, hold your hands in front of the animal, palms facing it, a few centimetres away.

✧ With either method, say:
Light of healing, flow and bring healing to my beloved animal.

✧ You may feel warm liquid flowing even more strongly through your palms and fingertips, and a sense of peace. Continue until you feel the energy fading.

✧ Wash the crystal under running water and keep it where it can absorb Sunlight and Moonlight until needed again. You can repeat the spell whenever necessary.

A regular absent healing spell for sick pets or animals who are ill treated or neglected

If you know of a sick animal or bird that needs healing, perhaps belonging to a family member or neighbour, you can send healing even if you live many miles away.

Most animal lovers are also concerned about animal welfare and can relate personally to any animal suffering. You may therefore regularly carry out this short, simple spell for animals in your local RSPCA and any domestic, farm or zoo animals that you know are neglected or ill treated anywhere in the world.

The more people who carry out a spell like this, the more powerful vibes are released into the cosmos to help the great number of abused animals. It is a good supplement to more practical ways of offering help.

You will need: A small notebook, a pink cloth, a pen, a pink candle and a pot of sage or thyme, or any herb or green plant.

Best time: Weekly if possible or whenever you have time. Work at the same time in the evening – 10pm is a good time for absent healing spells for animals as well as people. The spell takes only a minute.

The spell

✧ In your notebook write the name of any animal that needs healing or any local, national or international animal organisation you know that is caring for sick or neglected animals and birds. You can use a separate page for each.

✧ Choose a quiet place in your home. Put the pink cloth on to a flat surface or table, and place the book, candle and plant on to the cloth. Light the candle.

✧ Set the plant where the light will shine on it.

✧ Open the notebook at the first page and read each name or organisation in turn and say:
May he/she/they be healed by the power of light and love.

✧ When you have read all the names, add:
May all those animals and birds who are sick or suffering be healed by the power of light and love.

✧ Blow out the candle and visualise the light travelling to all the creatures that need it.

✧ Leave the plant and the book on the table. Open the book at a different page each day.

✧ You can take out the names of any animals that are healed or that pass away peacefully. If one dies, light the candle and speak a few words of blessing and thanks for the animal's life then blow out the candle and let the light find its way across the cosmos.

A spell for protecting all animals and birds in the wild

Whether you have a bird table, or enjoy watching videos about wildlife or visiting conservation parks, you can add your own magical spells for preserving wildlife and wildlife habitats for future generations. Many of these are under threat in the modern world.

Wildlife is important, not only for the balance of the ecosystem but as a heritage to our great grandchildren so that they do not have to go to the zoo or watch a video to know what a rabbit is. Indeed a recent survey suggested that some nine year olds could identify heroes from video games but did not know what a butterfly or sparrow was. You can focus the spell on your own favourite form of wildlife.

You will need: An open green space.

Best time: Any afternoon.

The spell

✧ Kneel down and touch the grass with your hands and knees. Say:

I connect. Protect all the creatures of the earth.

✧ Stand up and extend your arms upwards. Say:

I connect. Protect all the creatures of the air.

✧ Make a circle around yourself at waist height with your arms. Begin with your fingers touching in front of you and then extend your arms in a circle so that your hands briefly touch behind your back to complete the circle. As you do this, say:

I connect. Protect all the creatures of the waters.

✧ Touch next the centre of your brow, your eyes and then your ears and say:

I connect. I will protect the creatures of earth, air and waters with my mind and my awareness.

✧ Touch your mouth. Say:

I connect. I protect the creatures of earth, air and waters with my words.

✧ Touch your heart. Say:

I connect. I protect the creatures of earth, air and waters with my love and my concern.

✧ Finally clasp your hands in front of you. Say:

I connect. I protect the creatures of earth, air and waters with my actions. Protect me likewise, I ask.

✧ If you can, do something practical, join a conservation society or take friends and family to see good conservation parks where wildlife is cared for in natural surroundings and is encouraged to breed.

Chapter 12
Candles, Incenses, Oils and Crystals for Spell-casting

Some incenses and oils are multi-purpose: for example sage, sandalwood and lavender. In practice you can always substitute sage for an energising oil or incense, and lavender to soothe. But avoid sage in pregnancy (see page 4).

White candles can be used in place of others. You can use candles after spell-casting around the house unless you have been carrying out a binding or banishing spell. However, if you have filled a candle with energy it might be better to burn it in the dining room rather than the bedroom where the buzzing energies may keep you awake.

Clear quartz crystals can be substituted in any energising spell and rose quartz or amethyst in gentle, healing work. Alternatively, if you do not have the crystals listed you can use any that are the same colour as those suggested or substitute glass nuggets.

On the following pages I have summarised the spell topics and suggested candles, oils, incenses, crystals and the best day for creating spells (see pages 11–15 for how to make your own spells).

Home spells on Saturday

Candles

Pink for kindness and to create a peaceful atmosphere.

Brown for physical and emotional security.

Grey for casting protective barriers.

Oils and incenses

Freesia, lilac, lavender, lily, rose, sage and strawberry for a happy home.

Chamomile and rosewood for a calm household.

Patchouli, pine and lemon for domestic protection.

Crystals

Amethyst for protection against negative earth energies and ghosts.

Blue lace agate for peace and gentleness, jade and rose quartz for bringing love and healing sorrow.

Jet, obsidian, brown agate and brown jasper for strong defence of physical boundaries.

Happiness spells on Sunday

Candles

Orange for a clear identity and self-confidence.

Yellow for joy and fulfilment.

Green for self-love.

Pink for healing, especially of the spirit.

Oils and incenses

Eucalyptus, juniper, mint, sage and tea tree for health and vitality.

Rosemary and thyme for happiness and harmony.

Rose and ylang ylang for self-love.

Crystals

Amber and carnelian for self-confidence.

Boji stones and clear quartz crystals for the life force.

Jade and sugilite for harmony and gentle energy.

Kunzite and rose quartz, for self-love and healing of sorrow.

Relationship spells on Friday

Candles

Pink for gentle love, children, younger relations, harmony and forgiveness.

Brown for all domestic and practical issues and older family members.

Silver for mothers and grandmothers.

Gold for fathers and grandfathers.

Oils and incenses

Chamomile for gentleness and children.

Lavender for love and kindness.

Lilac and mimosa for all family matters.

Orange and sage for a secure family basis.

Rose for reconciliation and affection.

Rosewood for domestic harmony.

Crystals

Amber and amethyst and all brown stones, including banded agates, for stability.

Blue lace agate for softening criticism.

All jaspers and fossilised wood for general family matters.

Jade for children and peace at home.

Kunzite for adolescents.

Moonstone for women and mothers.

Obsidian for older people.

Rose quartz for children and healing.

Social spells on Monday or Tuesday

Candles

Orange for confidence.

Yellow for joy.

Green for family togetherness.

Pink for friends and reconciliation.

Red for injecting new life into your social world.

Oils and incenses

Apple blossom, avocado, bay, carnation, geranium, hyacinth, lavender, lily, marigold, mimosa and rose for family occasions, friendship and peace.

Ferns and ginger for excitement.

Orange for self-confidence.

Crystals

Blue lace agate, aventurine, jade, moonstone and rose quartz for kind words and honest actions.

Amber and carnelian for self-confidence.

Chrysoprase and coral for balanced emotions.

Obsidian for letting go of old and current resentments.

Clear quartz crystals, jaspers and malachite for positive but lively energies.

Love spells on Friday

Candles

Silver and green for attracting love, romance and fidelity.
Pink for gentle love and the rebuilding of trust.
Red for passion.
White for formal love rituals and major change points.
Silver for all Moon love spells.

Oils and incenses

Bay, basil and ivy for fidelity.
Cinnamon, ginger and rosemary for passion.
Lavender and rose for preserving love and gentleness.
Jasmine, mimosa and ylang ylang for sensuality.

Crystals

Jade and moonstones for first love and romance.
Rose quartz for gentleness and affection.
Garnets, emeralds and rubies for committed love.

Money spells on Wednesday

Candles

Yellow for an urgent or sudden need for money and for ventures involving speculation.
Green for the steady growth of prosperity.
Blue for the conservation of wealth.
Gold for major money-generating schemes or large amounts.

Oils and incenses

Allspice, basil, cinnamon and ginger for acquiring money fast.
Bay and patchouli for steady growth.
Frankincense, neroli and sage for bringing a new money source into your life and for grandiose schemes.

Crystals

Amber, tiger's eye and peridot for increased prosperity.
Metallic crystals such as haematite, lodestone and polished iron pyrites for all forms of money-making.
Silver, copper and gold, especially as coins, for instant and urgent money or for a gradual inflow of wealth.

Work spells on Thursday

Candles

Blue for all employment issues.

Yellow for jobs in technology or medicine.

Orange for the media, also anything to do with art or publishing and working with people.

Pink for working with children and animals.

Green for gardening or environment posts.

Brown for business, banks, civil service and government, and also for practical tasks where you will use your hands.

Oils and incenses

Allspice, cinnamon, eucalyptus and ginger for a new job or promotion.

Geranium, moss and vetivert for a happy workplace.

Lemongrass, parsley, patchouli, rosemary, sage and thyme for self-employment, new skills and growth of business ventures.

Crystals

Angelite/celestite, blue lace agate, kunzite and sodalite for a calm, happy working atmosphere.

Citrine, clear quartz crystals, lapis lazuli and falcon/hawk's eye (a blue version of tiger's eye) for a new job or promotion.

Amethyst, haematite, laboradite and malachite for protection against negativity. Malachite is especially good against adverse effects from computers and technological equipment.

Learning spells on Wednesday or Thursday

Candles

Blue for formal knowledge and examinations and tests of all kinds.

Yellow for increased memory, concentration and technological expertise, also for learning healing and alternative medical practices.

Brown for practical skills.

Oils and incenses

Eucalyptus, fennel and tea tree for learning new skills and technical expertise.

Frankincense for formal or long-term acquisition of knowledge.

Parsley, rosemary, sage and thyme for increased memory and concentration.

Sandalwood and pine for healing wisdom.

Crystals

Amazonite, carnelian and laboradite for confidence.

Citrine, crystal quartz, falcon's eye and haematite for focus, concentration and learning new skills.

Amber, desert rose and lapis lazuli for formal knowledge.

Candles, Incenses, Oils and Crystals for Spell-casting

Travel spells on Tuesday

Candles

Yellow for short-haul journeys, mini-holidays and air travel.
Blue for long-distance travel, long-duration stays and commuting.
Silver for journeys across water and for protection while travelling.

Oils and incenses

Basil, fennel and sage for protection while travelling.
Fern, frankincense and pine for all holiday spells.
Lavender and mint for trouble-free journeys and harmonious holidays.

Crystals

Amethyst, jet, smoky quartz, garnet and bloodstone for general protection while travelling and on holiday.
Sodalite for air travel.
Moonstone for travel by night.
Aquamarine for protection on the sea and when travelling overseas.
Turquoise to prevent accidents or attack while travelling. Turquoise is particularly good for animals in transit and for safe horse riding.

Animal spells on Saturday

Candles

Pink for healing.
Brown for older animals and for protection.
Green for endangered species and for love between owner and pet.

Oils and incenses

Mint, rosemary, sage and thyme rather than floral fragrances.
You can also make use of natural herbs.

Crystals

Earth stones such as brown and banded agates and smoky quartz for protection, soothing hyperactivity and for older animals.
Golden brown rutilated quartz and jaspers for energising.
Turquoise, the ultimate animal-protection stone, to prevent an animal straying, being hurt or stolen.
Jade for gentle energising as well as calming. Jade under a pet bed or placed in water before use can fill an animal with gentle energy or relax a hyperactive pet.

Index